A GUIDE
TO
COMPASSIONATE
CARE OF THE AGING

Other works by John Gillies

Novels
Antiochus (with Walter Price)
Martyrs of Guanabara

Nonfiction
A Guide to Caring for and Coping With Aging Parents
A Primer for Christian Broadcasters
Presbyterianism In Brazil (with Paul William Smart)

Children's Books
The U.S.S.R.—The World's Largest Country

Published Plays
The Retreat
The Sign Painter

Musical
The Firemakers (with David Seitz)

A GUIDE
TO
COMPASSIONATE
CARE OF THE AGING

John Gillies

Thomas Nelson Publishers
Nashville • Camden • New York

Published in Nashville, Tennessee, by Thomas Nelson, Inc. and distributed in Canada by Lawson Falle, Ltd., Cambridge, Ontario.

Printed in the United States of America.

Library of Congress Cataloging in Publication Data

Gillies, John, 1925-
  A guide to compassionate care of the aging.

  1. Aged—Services for—United States. 2. Social
work with the aged—United States. I. Title.
HV1461.G55   1985   362.7'0973   85-11514
ISBN 0-8407-5427-2

Contents

Part One
Meeting Basic Physiological Needs

Part Two
Meeting Basic Security Needs

Part Three
Meeting Basic Emotional Needs

79024

Part Four
Meeting Basic Esteem Needs

Part Five
Meeting Basic Growth Needs

Part Six
Meeting Miscellaneous Needs

Acknowledgments

Many people, in many places, have shared their time and experience with me, in person and by telephone and letter. I hope I have included all of their names. My wife, Carolyn, has participated in many of the interviews and has jogged my memory and perceptions in countless ways.

I am grateful to all of these good and caring people.

The survey form in Appendix A is taken from *How to Minister to Senior Adults in Your Church* by Horace Kerr, copyright © 1980 Broadman Press. All rights reserved. Used by permission.

Sister Patricia Murphy's suggestions for helping Alzheimer's patients (Chapter 6) first appeared in *Update* (Oct. 1984), the publication of the National Association of Activity Professionals. Used by permission.

This book is about the many ways people with good will, compassion, and imagination have found to make life more livable and worth living for our older friends. These are projects that work, projects that can be replicated almost anywhere.

1

Compassionate Care

Carolyn and I became caregivers ten years ago. My mother, Anna, was unable to continue living independently; we now know that she was a victim of Alzheimer's disease. My father-in-law, Paul Young, had a stroke, which left him both paralyzed and aphasic. During those ten years we learned the joys and the frustrations of caregiving. We experienced the entire spectrum of caring for loved ones—from home care, to supervised day care, to shared living facilities, to long-term nursing home care. That journey is described in my book, *A Guide to Caring for and Coping With Aging Parents.*

Anna and Paul, the care receivers, have died. But we are still caregivers. We still ponder what might have been. What if someone had intervened earlier in our parents' lives? What if some other alternative had been available, and tried? I have discovered that I am not alone in carrying this burden of "What if?" This continuing quest, this concern, perhaps even this residual guilt, is a legacy shared by a host of caregivers.

That gnawing, haunting "What if?" produced this book.

I knew that many of my friends faced the same problems and their aftermath. I wondered whether our community was typical of other communities. I was aware of the cutbacks in federal funding for social programs, many of these affecting the lives and well-being of older Americans. Were local governments or private agencies picking up their end of the "safety nets"? I knew there were alternatives to institutional care, but how well were they working? And what new, creative approaches were being tried?

11

Thus began a two-year study, researching gerontological journals and interviewing dozens of professionals and experienced volunteers. Here is an overview of what I found.

The Elderly Population

There is a significant elderly population, twenty-eight million, in fact. To understand the needs of these people, picture a group of twenty persons representing those who are sixty-five or older. Sixteen of the twenty (four out of five) manage their lives with little or no help. Four persons of the twenty require assistance of some kind, such as transportation, home-chore aid, and prepared meals. Only one of these twenty persons lives in a nursing home. Looking at this fact another way, only 5 percent of older persons live in long-term health care facilities. Surely the other nineteen merit more attention than they have been getting.

Some of these people are health impaired. One-half of the ten million Americans who need help with such daily activities as feeding, bathing, and dressing are older persons. They are not so severely handicapped that they require institutionalization, but, without assistance, they will likely be placed in institutions with consequent deterioration of their health and higher tax-supported medical costs for all of us.

Still others are abused. Yes, I said abused. We have become aware of child abuse in recent years. Now we need to come to grips with abuse of the elderly. In my state of Texas a thousand cases a month are reported. In Great Britain, it's called "granny bashing." There are even cases reported in Japan, where we expect exemplary respect for the elderly. There may be abuse of the elderly in your neighborhood and community—and it needs to be reported.

Some of the abuse is self-inflicted through self-neglect. Older persons may become very ill or suffer from Alzheimer's or some other memory-loss disease. They forget to eat or wash or take their medicine. They need to be referred to persons and agencies who can help them.

But there is also actual physical abuse of the elderly. Beatings and sexual assaults by younger members of the family are being reported. And the elderly are all too easy prey for thieves and sexual deviants. There is also emotional abuse by family members, such as food withheld as some sort of weird punishment for incontinence. There is financial abuse or exploitation, where a relative expropriates a social security check or abuses the power of attorney.

It is nasty business, but only as you know your community will you know if the nastiness, the cruelty, and the suffering exist. (For information on what to do or where to report such conditions, you should contact the Adult Protective Services branch of your state welfare or human resources department. In an emergency, contact the police.)

The private sector must enlarge and strengthen the safety nets for our vulnerable older citizens, since government resources for all kinds of social service programs are diminishing. Less money is coming from Washington, and state and local governments have not yet found ways to make up the difference.

We sometimes forget that the huge governmental social programs, so often criticized, are of relatively recent vintage. The Department of Commerce and Labor was only established in 1903 and divided in 1913. Illinois, in 1911, was the first state to provide assistance to mothers with dependent children. Child labor laws were enacted in 1916. The Social Security Act was signed in 1935 and is the source of many new "entitlement" programs. The Department of Health, Education, and Welfare (HEW, now divided into the Departments of Education and Human Services) was only established in 1953.

Who took care of orphaned children and the frail elderly before the government stepped in? The religious community established these caring programs, as well as public health and public education. And all along our frontiers, there was always a strong tradition of neighbors helping neighbors, whether it was rebuilding a barn or helping a family to survive. We must rediscover these roots of community compassion. Often we will find we have the human resources to make such programs possible.

Untapped Community Resources

Dr. Paul B. Maves, who is Director of Training for Shepherd's Centers International (see Chapter 12), looks at the statistics of the elderly in a novel way. He reminds us that 80 percent of the elderly are active and mobile. A fourth of them are actually gainfully employed! Dr. Maves calls them the "frisky" elderly. These older persons can serve as volunteers—and many do, often helping other elderly persons. Ten percent of older Americans are classified as "frail," people at risk and in failing health. The remaining persons are called "fragile," and need special assistance with daily living. But the frisky, venturesome elderly are in the majority and represent a tremendous human resource.

I am convinced that most older persons can live out their lives, with a little bit of help, in surroundings that can bring them joy and alleviate their loneliness. I believe that things can be done to help a large portion of our elderly population remain within the community. Institutionalization can be deferred and, in some cases, even avoided.

What we need is action. We need to become involved. The private sector is you and I—and our neighbors and friends and our church and community organizations.

Of course, it is easy for me to say, "Become involved!" Answering the question "How?" takes time and research. This book is my answer to your individual or your community or church group's question, "How can I (we) become involved?"

Let me begin by suggesting that you start with basic needs. None of us can function well if our basic needs are not met. For this reason, I have organized this book according to Dr. Abraham H. Maslow's need-hierarchy. Maslow created a kind of inverted pyramid, with basic needs at the bottom and growth needs at the top:

Self-Actualization
Self-fulfillment, achievement of potential, truth, goodness, beauty, aliveness, individuality, meaningfulness.

Esteem
Esteem of others and self-esteem; strength, achievement,
adequacy, confidence, independence, recognition.

Love
Affection, belonging, giving, and receiving
love.

Security
Protection from threat, danger,
illness; shelter, routine, order,
rhythm, predictability.

Physiological
Food, drink, sex, sleep;
activity, sensory
experience.

In Part One I will describe programs that deal with *physiological* needs: the basics such as food, drink, sleep, activity, and sensory experience.

Part Two moves up Maslow's pyramid to show programs that meet *security* needs: shelter, protection from illness and danger, and the need for order or predictable routine.

Part Three deals with the need for *love*: affection, a sense of belonging, the need to give and to receive love.

In Part Four we look at how to meet the needs for *esteem*. This includes self-esteem and the esteem of others, which are derived from a sense of achievement and adequacy, recognition and independence.

Finally, in Part Five we will consider the need for *self-actualization* or *self-fulfillment*. Persons are better able to achieve their human potential through various challenging activities and opportunities for learning. As you read through this book and research your community, you can move through this hierarchy of needs.

For instance, do the elderly in your community have a safe environment and eat hot, nutritious meals? Are older persons getting enough exercise? Next take a look at whether or not significant relationships are being fostered. Are they making new friends as older friends move away or die?

Quite often, groups that begin a "Meals on Wheels" program increase their involvement over the years to include programs that provide love, self-esteem, and self-actualization. The experts I have spoken to offer this advice: "Don't hurry this process. Concentrate on filling one need. Do this well. Then in a year or two, add a new program."

But before you can do anything, you must know the older people in your community. That's why I would like to suggest an essential first step in the process of compassionate care for the elderly: a survey.

First the Survey, Then the Plan

By now, you probably want to do more than just read about alternatives to nursing homes. You want to get moving. You want to go someplace. You want to do something for older people. Now!

Fine.

But please begin by getting some facts. Promise yourself not to start any program for at least six months. Promise yourself to use those six months to make surveys, to ask questions, to do research, and to explore resources.

For all of our joking about setting up new committees, there is value in several people working on a project, sharing information, and then formulating strategies. Call it a "work group," a "task force," or just a plain old-fashioned committee. It can help you to get moving responsibly.

And there is so much we need to learn. I suggest that you research these four different areas:

1. The Community of Older Persons

Start at the very beginning!

Learn about older people in general. Persons over sixty-five represent 11 percent of our population and get 29 percent of all health-care dollars. And yet, as already pointed out, four out of five older persons manage to live independently. This means that there are more older people living in your community than you realize.

Read about the issues of aging. My earlier book, *A Guide to Caring for and Coping With Aging Parents* (also published by Thomas Nelson), may be helpful. An excellent sound filmstrip called *Up Golden Creek* has been produced by the Presbyterians. It describes how life used to be for older people, why that life is less certain, why there are more elderly persons, what their impact is on housing and taxes, and why there are resentment and hostility toward the elderly. For information about purchasing this audiovisual, write: Presbyterian Office on Aging, 341 Ponce de Leon Ave., NE, Atlanta, GA 30365.

Other sources for helpful audiovisuals (many of which can be rented) are:

The Center for Studies in Aging, North Texas State University, Box 13438, NTSU Station, Denton TX 76203.

EcuFilm, 810 Twelfth Ave. S., Nashville, TN 37202 (also request their brochure, *Aging*).

Once you have reviewed the situation in general, turn to the particular. Who are the older people in your neighborhood or parish? What are their names? Where do they live? How many live alone? Are they handicapped? What are their needs?

Establish boundaries for your investigation. You cannot begin to meet all of the needs of all the elderly people in your city, or, perhaps, even in your area of the city. Choose a geographical area that is manageable.

Ideally, the information-gathering would be done by several groups in the same geographical area. These groups might be churches and synagogues, service clubs, or a combination of these groups.

Usually you need to take a survey or census to get this information, which requires lots of volunteer help. It also demands training for the volunteers. For example, interviewing is a skill that needs guidance and practice, and interviewing older people requires a special sensitivity.

The survey itself is something you can design or adapt from the sample survey at the end of this book (see Appendix A).

The best survey procedure is probably one that is an actual census—one that goes from door-to-door. But if this is not possible, given the area you choose and the number of helpers you recruit, the next-best method is to survey older persons in each congregation or group.

2. The Community of Your Church

You need to learn what groups or structures that serve adults already exist within your congregation, so you won't duplicate them. Include church school classes and adult fellowship groups. A survey with its own questionnaire will help to correlate information. (See Appendix A for a sample form.) Some of the questions you will consider are:

- What is the present organization and style of visitation programs?
- Do church officers have an assigned responsibility to visit elderly persons? If so, how often?
- Are church facilities used for community programs, such as Meals on Wheels?
- Is your church involved in any kind of a transportation program? Does it own a van?
- Are individual members participating in community programs? Or were they once involved, and no longer participate? (Knowing the depth and scope of the involvement of your members is important.)

This inventory will provide a foundation for expanded or merged programming, as well as a network for recruiting leaders to help develop new approaches.

It is also helpful to know what specific programs your own denomination administers for older persons. Check with your pastor and with your judicatory (conference, diocese, association, presbytery, etc.). So much has happened in this decade that your group may be pleasantly surprised with the studies, the resources, and the ideas that already exist—things that will facilitate your planning in the days to come. You'll need all the help you can get.

3. The Community

You need to know everything you can about organizations and programs already functioning in your city that have direct contact with older persons in your community.

Again, some kind of questionnaire or survey form will help in bringing together the data in a clearer way. The objective of this survey is to learn what is already being done that does not have to be duplicated. There is no need to reinvent Meals on Wheels, for example, if a viable delivered-meals program already exists.

Where do you begin?

Your committee probably knows of several organizations that should be visited.

There may be an Adult Services Council in your city. Your state may have a local office for its program for the aging. Your state may also have a Department of Community Affairs. There may be a local Council of Governments (COG) or a state Association of Regional Councils. These are primary sources for finding out about the specific organizations working on behalf of and with older persons.

If these sources are unavailable to you, check with local chapters of AARP (American Association of Retired Persons), the Gray Panthers, or RSVP (Retired Senior Volunteer Program, related to the federal ACTION program). You will also want to consult the federal Administration on Aging. (See Appendix D for the address of your nearest regional office.)

Learn all you can about local transportation and delivered meals programs, as well as adult day care centers. Such information will not only help you in your planning, but also in knowing which local agencies will be helpful if you develop a referral service.

People in these agencies are your colleagues; you are working together for a common cause. If you decide to begin a program of your own, you will want to visit these agency friends again (and again) for help and information.

4. Trends

Your committee should spend some time researching the dynamics and trends of your community and area. Let me suggest a few; you will find others that are specific to your own area.

There is a growing migration to the city from rural areas, and some of these newcomers are older people who have left places that were comfortably familiar. They now have to find new homes or places to rent at increasingly escalating costs.

Older people, who have been city-dwellers all of their lives and own their homes, are not as fortunate as they may seem. Inflation has raised the value of their homes and older homeowners find it more difficult to pay the ballooning higher taxes out of their fixed incomes.

If yours is a rural community, older persons living there are likely to be more isolated and may require more delivered services than their city cousins. But whether they live in the city or a small town, frequently older persons are not able to live with their children, since newer homes are smaller and there is no extra space for parents or other relatives.

Finally, there are still more widows than widowers because women live longer than men. And on the average women must manage with less income than men. Older women suffer significant financial hardship.

To be sure, there are many federal programs intended to help older Americans. However, these are "means-test" programs, which simply signify that these are programs with limitations. Very poor persons benefit from the built-in "safety nets" and supplemental income provisions. (In 1984, a person had to have a monthly income below $623 to qualify for such programs.) Middle class people have a special problem because of the income ceilings that have been established. A retired married couple whose combined retirement income is slightly above $18,000 a

year will not presently qualify for most of the special federally financed housing projects, for example. And yet $18,300 a year is
no longer a substantial income—not when you consider today's
taxes, prices, and health costs (especially long-term health care).

I have suggested that you take six months to make your study.
Perhaps you can garner the raw data in three months, but then
you will need the extra time to analyze that data and evaluate
your findings. Access to a personal computer may facilitate your
task. But a group working with newsprint or chalkboards can
achieve the same results.

Dr. Horace Kerr, the Southern Baptist leader of ministries to
senior adults, suggests a kind of homemade keypunch approach
to data processing. You can do this with any kind of form. Just
punch a hole beside each question in your survey. When you
tabulate results, punch another hole (or make a notch) beside
each "yes" answer. There should now be an open space at the
edge of your index card or sheet of paper. Now put your replies
together, thread a wire through the hole beside the question or
item you want to tabulate, and shake all of the cards downward.
The "yes" replies will fall through, and these can be quickly
counted. Then repeat the process for other questions. This technique can save time, especially with lengthy questionnaires.

Next Steps

After you have completed the study of your community, decide if the situation requires any action. If it does, then develop
viable, achievable goals with recommendations to the governing
body of your church, synagogue, or organization. If you can
suggest practical sources of funding for your recommendations,
you will be more successful in achieving your goals.

This book can be part of this second phase of your study because it describes what others have done, how they did it, and
what they would avoid doing if they could begin all over again.
There are also names and addresses for you to contact, in order
to secure more information about those projects that seem clos-

est to what will meet the special needs of older persons in your community.

Your "research and development" work will be important not only to today's elderly but to each one of us. As someone has said: "Aging is the one minority to which all of us will one day belong."

Part One

Meeting Basic Physiological Needs

2

Food
Providing Meals to the Frail
and Not-So-Frail

Among the several basic needs for humane human existence is food. Without the right kinds of food, there are malnutrition and illness, even starvation. Most older persons do not eat well nor wisely. My mother somehow survived on hot tea and white raisin bread while she was still living independently. I have no proof, but I think her physical and mental deterioration had its roots in poor nutrition.

Some popular mythology says that persons, as they grow older, require less food and sleep. Insofar as food is concerned, clinical studies demonstrate that while older people do not need as many calories as younger persons, they need the same amount of each essential nutrient. In her article, "Adequacy in Old Age, The Role of Nutrition," written some twenty years ago, Dr. Pearl Swanson, professor of nutrition at Iowa State University, explains why the right kinds of foods are so important for the elderly:

When food does not provide adequate amounts of the essential nutrients over a period of time, alterations occur in the composition of the fluids bathing all tissues in the body. Eventually there comes a time when the cells no longer can adjust to the alterations and a train of changes occurs that is reflected in the outward appearance of the individual, his behavior, his demeanor, his activity, his mental state, and his social and emotional reactions. It is significant that changes induced by poor nutrition are characteristic of those we associate with aging.

Ongoing metabolic processes demand that all essential nutrients be present simultaneously in the fluids nourishing the cells. The omission of even one nutrient makes it impossible for the body to maintain the sense, continuity and orderliness of its life activities. (*Journal of Home Economics*, Nov.-Dec., 1964.)

How does this happen? Why do the elderly suffer from or cause their own malnutrition?

One reason is economics. Most older persons live on fixed (and often reduced) incomes. Food budgets suffer. Shopping is a problem because of lack of transportation. Many older people will not or cannot travel the extra blocks or miles to take advantage of lower advertised supermarket prices. Even when an older person goes to a cafeteria, he or she is likely to choose food on the basis of the lowest cost.

Another factor is how food is made available in supermarkets. Except for some of the new "soup-for-one" cans or packets, food packaging is designed for family units, not individuals. Older persons are reluctant to spend money for food that can't be stored and may be wasted.

A third reason is social. When there is no one else to cook for or no one with whom to socialize and converse during a meal, the single elderly person often just doesn't care about preparing a warm, nutritious meal. This is why my mother drank tea and ate raisin toast. This is why at noontime I grab a snack instead of preparing something more nutritionally balanced, since I work and write at home, alone. I am delighted with several new cookbooks with recipes for two, which Carolyn and I use for our evening meals. But we do that because there is an evening meal to share.

There are other reasons for older persons not eating well. Some have ethnic backgrounds and can't get the foods they were once accustomed to. Others have dental problems and can't chew foods. Many are physically weak, or psychologically anxious or depressed, and have simply lost interest in food.

All of these reasons underscore the fact that food is important for the well-being of anyone—particularly for older persons. Community programs that provide healthy, nutritious food on a regular basis to the elderly are meeting an essential basic human need.

Such community programs provide either congregate or delivered meals, or both. We will look at several programs, varying in size and budget. Addresses are given for each program, if you wish more information. However, anyone contemplating the starting of a meals program should first contact the National Association of Meal Programs, P.O. Box 6344, Pittsburgh, PA 15212. It offers technical assistance in nutrition, recruitment of volunteers, fund-raising, and in securing equipment. This experienced clearinghouse can also put you in touch with a nearby program, which you could visit and observe.

Meals on Wheels
Summerville, South Carolina

This is a rather small program, providing and delivering about forty noon meals a day to frail and homebound residents. Summerville is located thirty miles northwest of Charleston and has a population of some five thousand persons. It is unique that this program, begun in 1981, uses no federal funds. Instead, funds are raised through contributions from civic organizations, businesses, and individuals. For instance, a church youth group secured sponsors for a hunger fast, which raised money for the project. Women of two churches combined efforts to create a quilt, which was auctioned for $2,000, benefiting the endeavor. Potential sponsors are told that $12 will provide hot lunches for an older person for one week, or $48 for a month, or $612 for an entire year. Finally, the county made a grant of $5,000.

Meal recipients don't have to pay a cent but are encouraged to make contributions. They must be sixty years old or older and suffer from some incapacity that prevents them from preparing meals.

The program requires a hundred volunteers (plus fifty back-up substitutes) to prepare and deliver the meals. Saint Paul's Episcopal Church provides office space and use of its kitchen to package the meals. The meals are prepared and purchased from the Presbyterian Home of Summerville.

"If these elderly people could not get home-delivered meals, many would not be able to remain in their own homes," states Jane Langston, once a volunteer and now the program's paid part-time director.

For more information, write: Meals on Wheels, P.O. Box 592, Summerville, SC 29483.

Meals on Wheels
Austin, Texas

The Austin program began in 1972 and is a much larger program than Summerville's. It is part of United Action for the Elderly, which in addition to Meals on Wheels also offers volunteer medical transportation, telephone reassurance, and a community awareness program for Austin's frail elderly persons. Its director since 1977 has been Jane Hammoud.

The program provides meals to 431 persons through thirteen sites (two are community centers, eleven are churches). Two meals are prepared for each recipient at each site on Monday, Wednesday, and Friday; one is packaged in a styrofoam container to be eaten on the day of the delivery, while the other is packaged in aluminum foil for reheating the following day.

A dietician prepares menus for a six-week cycle, which are followed in each preparation site. The menus are repeated only once during the year, which insures considerable variety. The meals are low sodium, low fat, and have no concentrated sweets; therefore, no special diets are needed, except for persons who have mastication problems (they are given a liquid food supplement such as Ensure).

The program requires dozens of volunteers (two to four at each site) and employs twenty-seven persons (thirteen are part-time). Each site has a coordinator who sees to it that food is available and recruits people to prepare and deliver it. Such a huge program requires a budget (in 1985) of $570,000, which includes some expenditures for equipment.

Support comes from federal funding through the Texas Department of Human Resources and from city and county sources. It is a United Way agency and is also related to Metro Ministries, an interchurch consortium. A Church World Service/ CROP Walk for the Hungry in 1984 designated 10 percent of its receipts for Meals on Wheels (the remainder going to a local food bank and to overseas projects fighting hunger). Recipients are charged a fee, on a sliding-scale basis, ranging from 50 cents a meal to $3. The Department of Human Resources reimburses the program for meals delivered to persons it has screened and approved.

In most cases, recipients must be fifty-five years or older; the exceptions are younger handicapped persons referred to the program by the Department of Human Resources. In all cases, the persons are unable to prepare a nutritious meal for themselves.

Referrals also come from churches, hospitals, and the Department of Human Resources. An application must be made which is verified by the program's own social worker and each potential recipient receives a home visit. The social worker assesses special diet problems and living conditions and instructs the client about the program (the time of delivery, the need to refrigerate the next day's meal, etc.).

Jane Hammoud says the greatest problem is administrative and deals largely with the delivery routes. There are three to seven delivery routes per site, with an average of eight persons receiving meals on each route. If someone isn't at home, that person's two meals go to a substitute. (A *substitute* is one of some 180 persons on a waiting list, who wait from three months to three years to get on the regular route, depending on the individual's need.)

The program also prepares an extra thirty-five meals each day for emergency needs. Often, a hospital will call to say that a person is being released who will need a delivered meal at home. Such emergencies will be covered for up to six weeks. If there are no emergency needs on a given delivery date, those meals go to the substitutes. There is no waste in this program. All prepared meals are delivered to someone who needs them. But obviously the logistics of managing this kind of delivery system in a large city can cause severe administrative headaches.

There is a constant need for volunteers, according to Hammoud. People move and have to be replaced, and there is a growing older population to be served; the program has grown 20 percent over a two-year period. People are living longer. And many older persons find the Sunbelt attractive for retirement, whether the move is affordable or not. One of the newest recruiting techniques is to get inner city office workers to volunteer their lunch hour for delivery of meals to inner city clients or to minority recipients who live on the fringes of the inner city.

For more information, write: United Action for the Elderly, Inc., P.O. Box 6235, Austin, TX 78762.

Congregate Meals

Gloria Mata Pennington, program manager of Senior Programs for the City of Austin, favors congregate meals for the elderly. "Those who are allowed to be 'homebound,' " she says, "will deteriorate faster." She delivers a few meals to private homes in her nutrition program, but does so reluctantly.

Her staff prepares 980 meals every day, Monday through Friday, which are delivered by vans to twenty-four different activity centers where they are served as the noon luncheon. Four of these sites are located outside of the city. Fifteen percent of the meals are delivered to private homes, but only with a physician's verification that a person is truly homebound.

"It's necessary to feed physical hunger," she says, "but there's a deeper hunger to be fed, the hunger to be with friends." She considers congregate meals to be preventive medication.

A *congregate meal* is simply a meal where people eat together, where they chat and visit while they eat. Congregate meals are usually provided in some kind of adult center, frequently the fellowship hall of a church, where the meal is preceded by programs and activities, including physical exercise.

The objectives are interaction and socialization. Pennington thinks that every effort should be made to get people who are homebound or roombound back into the mainstream of life. Otherwise, loneliness and depression set in, which affect nutrition and personal hygiene. "Get a person out of his or her home setting," she says, "and you'll see some dramatic changes." Friendships are made or renewed. Attention is given to personal grooming. Sometimes even a late-blooming romance occurs.

A program such as this is costly. There are sixty-nine employees—from cooks, to food service aides, to drivers for the vans who carry the food and drive the buses that bring the people. The annual budget is $2.5 million, allocated through the Parks and Recreation Department of the City of Austin. Federal money finds its way into this budget by way of Title III (b) for transportation and food (Older Americans Act).

Pennington admits that transportation is a key component to the success or failure of any program that combines meals with activities. It does little good to have a model program if people can't participate because they can't get there. Recent cutbacks in federal budgets have affected transportation more than nutrition programs.

Activity centers are discussed in much greater detail in chapters 4 and 6; but we should mention here that the activities that precede a noontime meal are more than fun and games, although there is some recreation. Help is given to older persons who struggle with the red tape of preparing applications or securing food stamps. Mini health clinics are held, aided by volunteer doctors and student nurses. Blood pressure is monitored. There is scheduled screening for oral and rectal cancer. And, as available transportation makes this possible, there are field trips to museums and other local places of interest.

There is no charge for a meal (which costs an average $2.15), but a "donation" of at least 25 cents is suggested. Most diners do contribute.

The meals are prepared in a central kitchen, which has a capacity for preparing fifteen hundred meals a day, and are transported to the twenty-four nutrition sites in specially designed thermal containers. Special trays are used in the centers, and elderly volunteers help with cleanup chores. Trays are returned daily to the central kitchen for steam cleaning.

"Seniors" also help with serving and wrapping napkins and silverware (plastic throwaways are not used). Other volunteers occasionally make favors for decoration of trays or tables.

Older persons have opportunity to voice their likes and dislikes about food, and menus often reflect such personal desires. However, meals are low sodium and rather bland. Condiments are provided at each center for those who prefer a little spice. The food is of such good quality that a local hospital requests it for its daytime dialysis patients.

For more information about this program, write: Senior Centers/Nutrition Sites, Austin Parks and Recreation Department, P.O. Box 1088, Austin, TX 78767.

Asbury Nutrition Program Site

For a look at an actual congregate meal site, we go to San Antonio, which has thirty-two such "nutrition sites."

Asbury gets its name from the Asbury United Methodist Church. Most sites are in churches.

The Asbury program began in 1975. The pastor, Wesley N. Schulze, heard about the possibility through what was then called the San Antonio Council of Churches. The city was trying to locate nutrition sites based on census tracts that showed where the majority of older persons lived. Asbury was right in the middle of one of these tracts.

The initial reaction of the congregation was, "What will this do to our building?" The attitude today is, "This is the most constructive thing we could have done with our building!"

The center opens at 9 A.M. (cooks arrive at 8), and persons often linger past lunch until 2 P.M. It serves a daily average of 110 persons, five days a week. There is no charge for a meal, but there is a contribution box. Guests may attend but they are charged for their meals.

Unlike the Austin operation, meals are prepared on site. Menus are provided by the Department of Human Resources on a rotating six-week cycle. Food must be secured from approved vendors. If a regular attendee becomes ill and is temporarily homebound, his or her meal will be delivered to the home.

A person must be sixty years old or older to participate. There is no financial means test (pegging services to poverty levels), but predictably most persons who come have limited incomes. They must register with the program and attendance is kept.

Food is important but the emphasis is on socialization. Pastor Schulze, now retired, says he witnessed significant changes in attitudes, appearance, and health. Many new friendships among these older persons were formed, and he even performed several weddings.

Activities include exercise, games, crafts, and field trips. There is frequent health screening. Speakers have included doctors, nurses, firefighters, and police officers, who discuss issues of health and safety.

About thirty-five volunteers assist the programs, helping with record-keeping, serving, programs, driving the van, and kitchen work. Five part-time persons were hired: a director, a cook, an assistant cook, a custodian, and a driver. Whenever possible, older persons are hired. The director is Paul Ader, a retired Air Force lieutenant-colonel.

The annual Asbury Center budget is $72,000. Funds for the citywide program come from the city and the state's Office On Aging (some 95 percent of funding actually comes from Washington). The Asbury United Methodist Church provides the building site but no money. It is reimbursed for utilities and purchases of food. In fact, the church benefited by acquiring equipment: a large freezer, two refrigerators, a commercial stove, and an institutional heavy-duty dishwasher. The church paid 11 percent of the total cost, with the understanding that after five years the equipment would become church property. The church was also assisted in the purchase of a van, which it uses to transport the elderly back and forth to its nutrition site.

Pastor Schulze and Mr. Ader have several suggestions for anyone beginning a congregate meals program.

If a clear need exists for such a program in a given neighborhood, offer your facilities as a "host station" to whatever local program may exist. Or, if yours is a small town and no program exists, your facility can begin a congregate program. In either case, you need a large assembly room and/or dining room and a kitchen. Make your location accessible for handicapped persons; add a ramp and grab bars in restrooms, if needed.

A house-to-house canvass will let older people know that this kind of facility exists for them. You can also prepare posters and handbills, and distribute these in supermarkets and laundromats. Visit community centers. Ask for word-of-mouth "advertising."

Leaders of congregate programs often encourage participation in service projects, since older persons themselves need to practice the grace of helping other older persons, especially those who are homebound and those who are roombound in nursing homes and hospitals. Programs and visits can be arranged. Thoughtful gifts can be made or sewn.

For more information, write: Asbury United Methodist Church, 4601 San Pedro, San Antonio, TX 78212.

Gardening for Health and Pocketbook

It is estimated that half of retirees grow their own vegetables. Increasingly, this is happening in "community gardens" with the cooperation of city and private organizations. Austin now has fifteen sites and is the largest community gardening organization in the Southwest. The gardens total twelve acres and are cultivated by seven hundred persons. One plot was an unused field next to the municipal airport. Another is on land owned by the state school for the blind.

One senior adult who benefited is R.T. Davis. At seventy-four years of age, he was weakened by a stroke and an unsteady heart, and spent his days watching television. Two years ago he learned about community gardening. He and his wife, Jodi, now work six 400-square-foot plots. They keep two freezers full of vegetables. Davis figures he saves several hundred dollars a year, and he is fairly sure that he has saved his life.

For more information, write: Austin Community Gardens, 2330 Guadalupe, Austin, TX 78705.

You might also want to contact Gardens For All, 180 Flynn Ave., Burlington, VT 05401. Its program includes special help for handicapped gardeners and a loan-bank of garden tools.

Two Food Projects from the West Coast

Food Advisory Service in San Mateo County is a mobile mini-market that brings groceries to more than five thousand elderly persons. Five vans are used in the nonprofit venture, delivering food to church social halls and senior centers. The seniors save 30 to 50 percent on their food costs.

In Santa Cruz, California, more than a thousand older adults arranged with local farmers to enter their fields and pick unmarketable produce. They call themselves the *Gray Bears*. These gleaners also receive free frozen food from area processors—packages that are either underweight or damaged. The city provides two employees and two part-time secretaries. Volunteers do the rest.

Afterthoughts about Food and Its Delivery

As you can see, Meals on Wheels programs vary. Some meals are prepared in large quantities and delivered to various stations for packaging and delivery to homes. In other places, the meals are prepared on site. Another variant is having the food prepared in quantity in a nursing home or hospital, then packaged elsewhere and delivered. In England there is a program that uses a large van as a kitchen-on-wheels; it goes from home to home and literally dishes out the hot food to older persons who need it. There is no one way of doing the job. But there is probably a best way of doing it in your community, a way that you will discover as you investigate and plan.

I once read about a program in Sweden that opened elementary school lunchrooms to older citizens at noontime. Menus were published in the local newspaper, so the adults could select a particular school. The oldsters had a special table and paid a modest fee for a good, hot meal. Mrs. Pennington tells me that this was tried in Austin and didn't work. "It sounds good in theory," she told me, "but most older people apparently feel that they raised their children a long time ago, and they can do without the stress and strain of children's chatter when they eat." I rather wish the theory might still be tested more extensively.

What do you cook if you get involved in either delivered meals or congregate meals? In most places, the menus and recipes will be given to you by a professional dietician. If you are "on your own," you might look for some large-quantity recipe books; a military source might be a place to begin. Or check with a hospital or a cafeteria. You might shop your bookstore for *Wenzel's Menu Maker*, second edition (Van Nostrand Reinhold Co.); it is comprehensive, very expensive, and designed for restaurant chefs. Your library may have a copy of a now-out-of-print book called *Better Food For Public Places* by Anne Moyer. And I have included some sample menus and recipes in Appendix B of this book.

There is also a simple way to adapt the recipes in your favorite family cookbook. Instead of doubling or tripling the recipe, determine how many servings you will need. Then you divide that number by the number of servings your recipe indicates. The answer is the factor you will use to multiply each ingredient of the recipe. Convert fractions to the nearest measure. Fractions of pounds should be converted to ounces, cups become tablespoons, gallons are now cups.

Example: You want to serve twenty people and your recipe says it will serve six. Divide 20 by 6, and your factor is 3.3. Multiply each ingredient of your recipe by 3.3. It is suggested that you not use this factor with seasonings. A little seasoning will go a long way.

The National Association of Meal Programs (see address at the beginning of this chapter) can help you locate the special kind of commercial equipment you may need, as well as suppli-ers of disposable products and containers for keeping food warm. Also write: The National Council on the Aging, Inc., 600 Maryland Ave., SW, West Wing 100, Washington, DC 20024. Ask for current information it may have on nutrition programs for the elderly.

I know that using military-style compartmentalized trays saves money, and these trays can quickly be steam-sanitized. I am also aware that plastic utensils and plastic (or paper) plates may be more efficient because they are disposable. And yet I wonder about the waste of petroleum that has made the plastic and the trees that have been converted to pulp to make the paper. Furthermore, I'm bothered by the lack of aesthetics. Surely there is a place, sometime, in congregate meal programs, to use stone-ware dishes and attractive flatware. (It doesn't have to be Spode china or silverplate!) The table might even have a floral center-piece. The environment could thus be made just a trifle more hu-man, and none of us would feel we were as disposable as the utensils we are using.

While I'm pondering, I also wonder why, when delivering meals to some handicapped or isolated person, someone—per-haps another volunteer—might not actually sit with that person and share a meal. Mealtime should be a time of sharing. There is so little celebration in our tightly structured programs.

And did you notice that the programs we have described are strictly Monday-through-Friday affairs? What happens on Satur-days and Sundays? And on holidays? Even in those cities where excellent nutrition programs for the elderly exist, there is a week-end gap that some churches or community organizations could and should fill. Food is a basic need—seven days a week.

3

Health
Innovations in Medical Response

Another basic need of the elderly is medical assistance. As you survey your community you will soon discover the handicapped and disabled, the blind, and the hard of hearing. You will see those who are obviously frail and at risk, perhaps due to arthritis. More investigation will be needed to learn who are diabetic or have high blood pressure or thyroid problems.

Older persons who live independently often develop serious nutrition-related illnesses. Or due to confusion or memory-loss diseases, they may overmedicate themselves or sample everything in the medicine cabinet—or forget to take prescribed medications. Someone needs to monitor such situations. Someone often needs to be available to provide the transportation that older persons need in order to get to clinics for laboratory tests, to see their doctor, dentist, or podiatrist.

Visiting nurse associations or public health services help. So do the personnel of adult day health care centers, discussed more fully in Chapter 6. Your task may be simply to make referrals, to put older persons who are in need of medical help in touch with existing agencies.

However, there are special ways communities can help with medical needs of the elderly.

Medical Identification

The National Safety Council has developed a unique "Health ID," the size of a credit card, which is kept in one's wallet. Medical and other vital information is recorded on a microfilm strip about the size of a postage stamp, which is placed on one corner of the card. A tiny magnifying glass is laminated to the other corner. In case of an emergency, the doctor or paramedic bends the card so that the lens is over the microfilm. Placed against a light, the essential medical facts of the person can quickly be determined.

A tremendous amount of information can be placed on the microfilm. This might include major ailments, allergies, medications, the date and address of the most recent hospitalization, blood type, name and telephone of physician, people to contact in an emergency, use of contact lenses or dentures (which should be removed if a person is unconscious), and insurance information (health, Medicare, and auto). The document has room for authorizing permission for surgery and even a baseline electrocardiogram reading. The latter could save a life in case of a heart attack. Stickers are provided for windshields, wallets, and telephones to alert others in an emergency that the person has such a medical ID card in his wallet or her purse.

A lady from Florida was traveling in Alaska when her erratic driving caught the attention of a state trooper. He pulled her to the side of the road and became alarmed when she could not respond to his questions. He drove her to the nearest hospital. The doctors could not determine what was wrong until the woman had the presence of mind to pull out her medical history card. It stated that she had a chemical imbalance that required a certain medication. Her condition stabilized after she was given the drug, and she continued her trip.

The National Safety Council recommends that persons with serious medical problems also wear a bracelet or medallion, giving essential medical information. One such medical alert system is the nonprofit Medic Alert organization. It provides a metal emblem, worn on wrist or neck, which describes the wearer's problem in a few words and lists a file number and a toll-free telephone number to call for complete medical information.

An excellent project in your community would be to secure such medical information data for each older person.

For information regarding applications and fees, write:

National Health and Safety Awareness Center, National Safety Council, 333 N. Michigan Ave., Chicago, IL 60601.

Medic Alert Foundation, P.O. Box 1009, Turlock, CA 95381.

Emergency Response Systems

These are literal lifelines for the older adult living alone. Using telephone lines, this new technology links the home with a medical center. It provides security around the clock. If a client signals for help, someone calls back within seconds to learn more about the situation. The center may dispatch a volunteer or contact an ambulance service, the fire department, or the police.

This type of service is especially valuable in the event of heart attacks, strokes, falls, emotional stress, robbery, or assault. An automatic timer provides extra security by sending a help call if the client is unconscious and can't use the button. If the timer isn't reset daily, the medical center is automatically notified of an emergency.

You may be able to encourage a local hospital or nursing home to establish such a system. For information, contact Lutheran Social Service of Texas, P.O. Box 49589, Austin, TX 78765-9589, which offers such a service. A commercial firm marketing this type of emergency service is American Health Monitoring, Inc., 3198 Oakcliff Industrial St., Atlanta, GA 30340. Telephones designed for the hearing and speech impaired are manufactured by Plantronics, 345 Encinal St., Santa Cruz, CA 95060.

Of course, *telephone reassurance programs* can accomplish some of the same objectives. Volunteers "adopt" an older person whom they telephone every day at an agreed-upon time. The calls provide friendly contact but they can do more: persons can be reminded to take certain medications or a quick assessment can be made of a person's emotional state. If no one answers at the regularly scheduled time of call, an emergency may exist. No special equipment is needed. What is needed is someone to recruit volunteer callers and link these with older persons who will benefit from this service. Each person uses his or her own telephone. It isn't round-the-clock lifeline technology, but it could be the start of something that can be helpful as the program grows. For information about a local telephone reassurance program, write: United Action for the Elderly, P.O. Box 6235, Austin, TX 78762.

A SWAT Team

SWAT in police terminology means a "special weapons and tactical" team. In an innovative program in Miami Beach, Florida, *SWAT* means "Service Workers Action Team." (The original name, "Service Workers for Aged in Trouble," was vetoed by the older persons for whom the program was designed.)

Miami Beach is a haven for the elderly, most of whom live in hotels or apartment buildings of varying size and vintage. The Miami Jewish Home and Hospital for the Aged—drawing upon earlier experiences of New York City's Montefiore Hospital and a geriatric psychiatric team in Norristown, Pennsylvania—decided to develop its own "delivered services" program to persons in its beach community who were sixty years old or older.

A secondhand recreational camper was renovated to serve as the base of operations in the field. An examination table was installed, as well as radio communications equipment and a computer terminal linked with its main office. The camper's refrigerator and stove would allow for emergency meal preparation and delivery.

The team initially included a program coordinator (an MSW—an experienced person with a Master's in Social Work degree), an administrative assistant, a clinical social worker, a chore worker, a home health aide, a nurse trained in geriatric procedures, a support staff member (who doubled as a driver and clerk), and a part-time vocational counselor. The vocational counselor was subsequently dropped from the team but a second chore worker was added.

The team established these goals: to assess the functional status of the elderly, to prepare individual care plans, to deliver a variety of services to the individual's home (including health and

mental health, homemaker, chore, nutrition, and health education services, and therapies), and to provide continued monitoring of each prospective "client."

The team chose ten buildings in Miami Beach, visited each
apartment, left descriptive pamphlets, and invited residents to a
social function. The plan was then explained to the senior residents and suggestions were encouraged.

A newsletter was prepared for each building, listing scheduled
activities during the weekly visit of the SWAT team. In some
buildings, the team would spend an entire day, while a half-day
might be sufficient in others. However, certain members of the
team might return to help a specific person several times a week.
Ongoing counseling for a person in distress or depression might
be required. A chore worker might be needed on a daily basis after an elderly resident returned from a hospital stay.

Here is a sampling of what happens during a regularly scheduled weekly team visit. A dental hygienist might be scheduled for
9 A.M. There would be exercises at ten. In the afternoon, a lecture
on proper use of medications would be arranged. Other speakers would come to talk about safety and security in apartments,
or a politician might be invited to discuss an issue or legislation
affecting older persons. During the rest of the day, the SWAT
team would visit with individuals, providing services or referring
persons to other agencies.

The SWAT program received funding for three years, beginning in 1979, from the Administration on Aging. Its annual
budget was $165,000. For more information, write: Miami Jew-
ish Home and Hospital for the Aged, Douglas Gardens, 151
Northeast 52d St., Miami, FL 33137.

Delivered Medical Services in a Rural Community

The lone doctor in rural Hopkinton, Rhode Island, retired in
1976, and residents of four communities were left without medical care. The nearest hospital was twenty miles away. So Brenda
Pukas, a local nurse, met with residents and planned a health
maintenance program for the four towns. She began a center,

the Wood River Health Services, in a small converted grocery store. A physician commuted two evenings a week for consultations. Daily assistance was provided in the areas of medical, nutrition, dental, family planning, and counseling services.

In 1981 the center moved to a new six-thousand-square-foot building where doctors were available twelve hours a day. The thirty-person staff helped persons of all ages who were able to come to the center. However, it was soon clear that special services were needed for older persons who were mobility-impaired and isolated. A grant through the Rhode Island Department of Elderly Affairs helped to establish a separate program of delivered services to older persons.

The team learned that the rural elderly lived in old homes that are expensive to heat and maintain. Many of these older persons were too frail to manage their vegetable gardens, but their incomes were just high enough to make them ineligible for many federally funded programs. The team discovered significant medical needs but also found that these older persons had serious emotional and financial needs. They needed emotional support to deal with loneliness. They required intellectual stimulation. And they could be helped with information about tax rebates, fuel aid, and Medicare.

The program now functions on a reduced basis, due to federal funding cutbacks, but information about the current program may be secured by writing Wood River Health Services, Route 3, Hope Valley, RI 02832.

Geriatric Medicine

In 1982 one-third of all medical schools in the United States offered courses in geriatrics. That's the good news, because a decade ago less than a dozen medical schools included such studies in their curriculum. The bad news is that only 2 percent of medical students took advantage of the opportunity, since geriatric studies are optional.

An exception is the Gerontology Internship Program at Cornell University Medical College in New York City. The six-week program is intensive and is required of second-year medical students. Nineteen participated in the 1984 session. It may be the only such program in the United States.

The students work out of five neighborhood social agencies. They visit older people in their homes and help them with the complicated paperwork required for medical and other benefits. They run errands, help people with check cashing, bill paying, and banking. They arrange for medical and dental visits. They become acquainted with government bureaucracy by standing in line on behalf of their patients at various government agencies.

The project is coordinated by the medical school's public health department. One objective is to "give medical students some exposure to old people who are not lying half-dead in hospital beds," according to Alice Ullmann, clinical associate professor of social work in the medical college.

Dr. Hirsch S. Ruchlin, professor of economics in public health, says, "Older people have too often been dealt with in a lecture hall and not in real life. Doctors need to change their mind-set and focus not simply on diseased organs, but on a person who exists in a social environment."

This type of program requires substantial financial aid. Students receive a $1,500 stipend for the six-week program, provided from two trust funds.

You might want to check with your nearest medical school to see what courses and opportunities are offered to better prepare doctors for helping older patients. Perhaps you could be a catalyst for finding the funds that might help such programs become a reality.

For more information, write:

Cornell University Medical School, 1300 York Ave., New York, NY 10021.

The American Academy of Family Physicians, 1740 W. 92d St., Kansas City, MO 64114.

Hospices

When a person is incurably ill, conventional medical treatment may no longer serve any useful purpose. A happier alternative may be a hospice.

In the Middle Ages, a hospice was a place of shelter for travelers and for ailing or dying pilgrims. (The Latin word *hospes* means "guest.") The modern hospice movement began in 1967 when Dr. Cicely Saunders opened Saint Christopher's Hospice in London. The first hospice in the United States was established in New Haven, Connecticut, in 1974. Ten years later, in 1984, there were an estimated twelve hundred hospice programs in North America.

The hospice approach focuses on the daily physical, spiritual, and psychological needs of the patient and his or her family. The hospice program neither hastens nor postpones death. A hospice seeks to help terminally ill persons live out their lives as fully and as comfortably as possible.

The approach requires a team of persons of varied expertise and experience, combined with great sensitivity. There are several models of providing service, but the providers always represent medicine, nursing, social work, and clergy.

The hospice facility may be located in a hospital or in a private home; or a local hospice service may be a combination of both hospital and home. If lodged in a hospital, the hospice section will occupy a separate wing with special staff. If lodged in a private home, family members are encouraged and enabled to meet needs there. Hospital-type beds and other equipment are secured. If a patient has no family, neighbors or other volunteers are recruited and trained to be part of this special support system. Hospice care is usually under the guidance of the patient's own physician who is responsible for the management of pain.

There are two hospice programs in Austin, Texas. One is operated by a local health service provider (Girling's, Inc.), which provides interdisciplinary team care in homes only. Its charges are on a sliding-scale basis. (Medicare reimbursement is now available, and private health insurance carriers are beginning to include hospice services in their benefit coverage.)

Another, called *Hospice Austin*, which describes itself as a "comprehensive program," offers the team approach and trains volunteers to work with the terminally ill and their families. It not only maintains a relationship with four local hospitals but also provides home care. It makes no charge for its services and is supported by grants and contributions. At any given time, twenty to thirty persons will be served in the hospitals and fifteen to twenty in individual homes.

To initiate a hospice program requires the widest possible community communication with physicians, nursing and social services, and clergy. A first step would be to secure information and guidelines from the National Hospice Organization, Suite 402, 1901 North Fort Myer Drive, Arlington, VA 22209.

Training Companions and Health-care Paraprofessionals

An important cog in the health services delivery wheel is the individual who can assist family caregivers, whether in the hospital, nursing home, or private home. Often a registered nurse or a practical nurse is not required, but someone with some special health-care skills can be of great help.

Good, qualified people are hard to find. Carolyn and I certainly found this to be true when we provided home care to our parents. Health-care agencies advertise a full spectrum of help—from R.N.s to chore helpers—but except for medical professionals there doesn't appear to be much standardization when it comes to qualifications and skills. There can be a lot of learning by trial and error, but that kind of learning is hard on the patient.

Community agencies are beginning to do something about this need. Most seem to be recruiting persons fifty-five years old or older, and all have specific programs of training which must be completed.

A new program in Austin is called *S.S.S.*—Senior Sitter Service. It requires twelve hours of intensive training which goes far beyond mere "sitting." It intends to provide an in-home respite care program for spouses and families who are presently caring for frail or disabled elderly persons. For additional information, write: SSS, Inc., 5002 Tahoe Trail, Austin, TX 78745.

Companions for Recovery Program

The Upper Cumberland Area Agency on Aging in Tennessee has had several years of experience in developing its *Companions for Recovery* program, which covers a fourteen-county area.

Mona Rector, developer of the program, says that 40 percent of the trainees, who are fifty-five years old or older, have less than an eighth grade education and have never had a chance to do anything in the health field, even though they have wanted to be in health care. "They make excellent companions," she says, "because they are mature people and have a wealth of experience to begin with. They've reared their own family and have cared for family members." Rector has trained 315 people over a period of thirty months, and 85 percent of those are employed.

The training is extensive. It requires a commitment to give sixty hours over a two-week period. The course costs $25 and includes the text *Being a Homemaker/Home Health Aide* by Elana Zucker (Prentice-Hall).

The course includes practical work in the home, simulating full bed-bath, changing an occupied bed, and transferring a patient, along with measuring and recording vital signs. There are sessions on nutrition and medication, fire safety, and job survival skills. Audiovisuals on first aid, heart attack and stroke, cancer, and home safety are shown and discussed. It is a minicourse in practical nursing, without the license or certification.

The agency doesn't guarantee anyone a job, but does provide names of graduates to all health facilitators in the fourteen-county area. Graduates negotiate their hours and salary with potential employers. Rector says most of the jobs are short-term; companions help a family in the hospital, or later in the home. Patients recover, or they deteriorate to the point where long-term professional health care is needed, or they die. But, she says, graduates are kept busy. For most of them, this is an important new source of income as well as personal accomplishment and satisfaction.

Rector doesn't do it all by herself. Personnel from hospitals, health departments, and home health agencies assist her in teaching. She looks for schools, churches, or nursing homes to serve as classrooms. These are good clues for you to pursue. And you can secure more information by writing the Upper Cumberland Development District, 1225 Burgess Falls Road, Cookeville, TN 38501. Ask about the "Companions for Recovery" program.

OASIS

OASIS (Older Adults Sharing Important Skills) is a program to recruit, train, and supervise volunteers who will work as mental health paraprofessionals in nursing homes. It is based in Bryan/ College Station, Texas, the home of Texas A&M University. The program is sponsored by the university's Department of Educational Psychology, the Texas Agricultural Extension Service, and the Retired Senior Volunteer Program of Brazos County.

Thirteen volunteers, all of them fifty-five years old or older, completed the six-month training program (involving six to ten hours per week) in 1984. Ten persons were recruited for the second training event in 1985. Smaller classes assist the learning and sharing process. All thirteen of the first graduates are actively using their new skills in local nursing homes.

The volunteers are motivated by a desire to help meet the emotional needs of the institutionalized elderly. They learn basic counseling skills and become familiar with the physiological and emotional aspects of aging, as well as with problems that are peculiar to nursing home residents. They learn to identify different emotional needs and effective ways to meet them.

I asked Royda Crose, coordinator of the program, to evaluate the first year's experience. She was cautious, saying that volunteers bring a variety of experiences and skills. Some, she says, have not really gone beyond being a "friendly visitor," emphasizing that this is not unimportant. She rates four of the thirteen volunteers as competent paraprofessionals, who work not only with residents but also with their families.

Crose believes that for the program to be successful, volunteers should (1) be emotionally healthy themselves and (2) have the time to give to the program. A person needs to be able to visit nursing home residents at least three times a week; once a week just isn't enough.

The work of the volunteers is evaluated by staff; but Royda Crose is especially pleased that the volunteers themselves have established their own support group, where they share their experiences and concerns. She feels this is a hopeful indicator for future success.

Nursing home residents endure a lot of loneliness and depression. Their families are often frustrated and guilt-ridden. Mental health paraprofessionals who establish friendly rapport with resident and family can make a great contribution to the well-being of both. The volunteers benefit by learning new skills and personal growth.

To begin such a program in your community, consult with Mental Health/Mental Retardation persons, as well as with educational psychology departments of local or regional colleges and universities. Include RSVP or similar action-oriented older-adult organizations. And write PROJECT OASIS, Educational Psychology Dept., Texas A&M University, College Station, TX 77843. (You may want to refer to Chapter 13, and the description of the peer counseling program called PACE.)

Exercise and Other Programs

In California some volunteers developed a program called *SAGE* (Senior Actualization and Growth Exploration). It is based on the concept of deep muscle relaxation: first of body, then emotions, and finally, of mind. Deep breathing is the basic "exercise," and traditional exercises are geared to the capacity of the members. Many claim relief from physical aches and pains. Others have found release from emotional tensions caused by grief.

In Arlington, Virginia, a sixteen-week *Health Activation Course* helps the elderly to accept more health-care responsibility for themselves. They are taught when it is appropriate to consult a doctor and how to ask the right questions when they do so.

Things to Do

Check with health clubs in your area to see whether special programs—and discounts—are available to senior citizens. If not, encourage the management to give this serious consideration.

Several excellent exercise records and cassettes designed for the elderly are available for use with groups or with individuals. For information, write: Homebound Resources, Ltd., P.O. Box 180082, Austin, TX 78718.

To become better informed about the various federal entitlement programs, consult Appendix C or contact the office of your member of Congress.

4

Activity
You're As Old As You Feel

Among the basic physiological needs of older persons are the needs for activity and sensory experience. A primary way of meeting these particular needs is through the *multipurpose senior center*. A parallel but quite different program is the *adult day care center*, which is dealt with separately in Chapter 6. (The significant difference relates to the word *care*; senior centers do not provide supervised care while adult day care centers do.)

The multipurpose senior center is defined as a community facility in which older people may come together to fulfill many of their social, physical, and intellectual needs. The center is also a bridge, linking the senior community to the community at large. Most congregate meal sites, or nutrition sites, maintain a senior center along with a meal program. Thus, *multipurpose* may be understood as something beyond "activity" or "fun and games." Nutritious meals are served, and multipurpose senior centers offer a variety of significant services.

Such centers have a relatively recent history. The concept of the senior center probably began in Cleveland, Ohio, in the 1930s. The Golden Age Club was organized there by Oscar Shultze, an immigrant social worker, under the auspices of the Benjamin Rose Foundation. Shultze observed that older persons gathered in parks and railroad station waiting rooms, and he felt something better could be provided.

The William Hodson Community Center was begun in New York City in 1943 and was the first facility known as a senior center. It was started because social workers sensed that many eld-

51

erly persons sought extended opportunities for communication and conversation. A center would alleviate their loneliness and fill their leisure time. And so the Hodson Center was begun in temporary quarters and soon attracted 350 persons. That number quickly decreased to about forty, as the center turned into a kind of social club for its more forceful, domineering members. Professional staff was secured to stimulate ideas and cooperation, and the club once again became a community center. It continues to function and is now sponsored by the New York City Social Services Department.

A San Francisco senior center was started near Fisherman's Wharf in 1947, funded by United Way. Another West Coast facility opened in Menlo Park, California, in 1949, the same year that the Philadelphia Center for Older People began. These were the pioneers. They offered a full recreation and education program, and provided guidance and counseling. The Philadelphia center brought in sewing machines and ironing boards—and even provided free showers.

Dr. Paul Maves, a consultant on ministries with the aging, points out that by the 1950s many churches had picked up the "club" idea, providing space for meetings. Often these were funded by a city's Parks and Recreation Department. Dr. Maves observes that, "After all, this was just another version of the organized Adult Bible Class and the Luncheon Club."

The idea of senior centers finally blossomed with the passage of the Older Americans Act in 1965 (amended in 1973). The National Council on the Aging in 1970 added the National Institute of Senior Centers to its roster of service agencies. In 1971, the White House Conference on Aging devoted six of its conference sessions to planning for expanded development of senior centers. At the present time, there are more than eight thousand senior centers throughout the nation.

Let's look at the kinds of services that are offered in a senior center.

There are counseling and referral services. Older persons have someone with whom to discuss personal problems. They can learn about persons and agencies who can help them with matters relating to health, housing, safety, legal aid, and finances. Qualified people help them with their income tax forms.

There is assistance with employment, as healthy older persons are encouraged to find part-time or full-time employment. The center is a clearinghouse for information about community resources and job opportunities. Workshops are held to help people refresh their job-hunting skills, particularly interviewing techniques.

Some centers establish a food cooperative, staffed by members, which provides income and savings.

Services are provided to the homebound. Center members serve as friendly visitors and shopping aides or participate in a telephone reassurance program.

Health maintenance programs and geriatric screening clinics are provided.

Centers provide special vehicles to transport senior citizens to libraries and museums, as well as to clinics and shopping centers. These services extend beyond the individual. Groups are offered opportunities in camping, crafts, and trips. A noontime nutritious meal is provided. Discussion groups and other educational events are organized. And, of course, special holidays and members' anniversaries are commemorated with parties and other events.

We have twenty-four senior centers in Austin, four of these located outside the city in Travis County. The majority of them are located in churches. However, several recreation centers, designed for multigenerational use, are utilized. And a handsome free-standing Senior Activity Center was completed several years ago, which is used exclusively by older persons. The building makes a statement that the city of Austin takes its senior citizens seriously, providing facilities that are specifically designed for their use. The program is sponsored by the city's Parks and Recreation Department.

Fort Worth (and Tarrant County) also has twenty-four senior centers, administered by a United Way agency called Senior Citizen Services. It provides information and referral assistance, transportation, trips and tours, health services, recreation, meals, educational opportunities for personal growth and enrichment, and outreach through volunteer service and visiting the elderly homebound. This is truly multipurpose, and its program is similar to that of other senior centers.

The Presbytery of Indian Nations sponsors a community center in Oklahoma City, housed in the former Second Presbyterian Church. In addition to a senior center and a nutrition site, there are a food bank, a clothes closet, and a day care center for children. The First Korean Presbyterian Church also worships in the facility.

One of this community center's major projects is the restoration of residences in the neighborhood. This not only increases the value of property, but helps to keep the multiracial and multiethnic community more stable.

Transportation is another important part of its program. Oklahoma City is the third largest city in land area in the United States, and its public transportation system is limited.

For information about these three programs, write:

Senior Programs, Parks and Recreation Department, P.O. Box 1088, Austin, TX 78767.

Senior Citizen Services, 1000 Macon St., Fort Worth, TX 76102.

Presbyterian Community Center, 1008 North McKinley, Oklahoma City, OK 73106.

Persons must be fifty years old or older to participate in a senior center program, which says something significant about the purpose of senior centers: to prepare persons in midlife to begin to adapt themselves to a changing lifestyle. These are healthy, vibrant people who establish new friendships while still in their preretirement years. Such friendships will last into retirement. Patterns are established that help aging persons to keep active physically and mentally.

Sponsors are either public or private. Public sponsors are state, county, or city. Usually these are either departments of recreation or social services. Private nonprofit sponsors may be the local Salvation Army, a Jewish community center, YM/YWCAs and YM/YWHAs, churches, family service agencies, settlement houses, or homes for the aged. Unions have sponsored senior centers—notably the United Auto Workers and the Amalgamated Clothing Workers. The United Way is also a source of funding.

The senior center was defined earlier as being a "bridge." It offers an opportunity for older persons to become involved significantly with their own community. This occurs through social service, as older persons volunteer their work in hospitals or schools. It also occurs through social action. Older persons contact their legislators. They participate in city council meetings, often helping to secure a stop sign at some dangerous intersection, or sharing their insights about the encroachments of development.

It is easier to begin a multipurpose senior center than an adult day care center for several reasons. Licensing is not required in most states because medical services are not provided (nor needed). Fewer staff persons are hired. The program day is shorter. And members are physically and mentally able to assume much more responsibility for planning and programming.

Veteran senior center planners offer the following suggestions to newcomers to the field:

(1) Secure as broadly based sponsorship as you can. This will attract a greater range of participants. A single community group can be a sponsor, of course. But experience says that "more is better."

(2) Incorporate under the appropriate state law as a *nonprofit* or *not-for-profit* corporation (the precise term may be significant in your state). Also, file an application with the Internal Revenue Service for exemption from federal taxes as a "*501 (c) (3)*" organization. Such tax-exempt status does not automatically follow nonprofit incorporation. Seek the advice of an attorney with state corporation law experience. Incorporation and IRS registration may secure exemption from property and sales taxes. It also allows donors to claim exemption from federal income tax for contributions made to your organization. It allows you to secure lower postal rates (consult with the permit section of your local

post office for information and necessary forms).

(3) Choose a location that is central and convenient to public transportation or where there is safe and accessible off-the-street parking.

A shopping mall site might be an ideal location. A mall is enclosed and weatherized. There is a lot of room for walking. There are shops and shoppers to observe. Perhaps an advantageous deal could be negotiated with mall management for one of its vacant shops.

In Elkmont, Alabama (population 429), the citizens restored its old railroad depot, converting it to a senior center with federal funds. The depot also houses the town library and a kitchen to prepare meals for its Meals on Wheels program.

(4) Visit your nearest senior center. Ask questions about the program, the kind of staff needed, organization, budget, and funding. Observe the operation. Participate in it.

(5) Join the National Institute of Senior Centers. Its updated publications define standards, offer architectural designs, and provide many management tools not available from any other source. It publishes a bimonthly newsletter. It offers seminars, workshops, and management training. Your membership also includes affiliation with the National Council on the Aging.

(6) Keep in mind that senior centers are designed for the healthy, independent older adult. The centers, however, can turn into close-knit clubs. There is a place for this kind of fellowship and activity, of course, but cliquishness does not help the stranger, especially the handicapped person who may wander in. Carolyn's dad, Paul, attended a senior center for six months. At first, the regular "members" looked askance at his wheelchair and paralysis. In time, they accepted him and even found ways to communicate with Paul, despite his aphasia. But it did take time.

For information about membership and resources, write the National Institute of Senior Centers, The National Council on the Aging, Inc., 600 Maryland Ave., SW, West Wing 100, Washington, DC 20024.

Part Two

Meeting Basic Security Needs

5

Housing
There's No Place Like Your Own Home

One of the most basic human needs in life is the need for safe, secure shelter. This need is especially acute for older persons. According to a recent University of Michigan study, it is estimated that 235,000 additional housing units per year will be needed by the year 2000 for the growing population of persons over sixty-five years of age. But we dare not wait until the turn of the century to attack this need. Older people need adequate, affordable housing now.

Retired persons on low fixed incomes pay a greater percentage of their incomes for housing than those with larger incomes. That may appear to be obvious, but consider: low-income renters often pay more than 35 percent of their monthly income for rent, while high income renters pay as little as 11.6 percent. There is an eighty-two-year-old widow in my city who has rented the same home for sixteen years. Her rent has been increased from $300 to $400, which is 57 percent of her monthly income of $700.

The supply of affordable rental housing is not increasing to meet the demand of persons with minimal or even moderate incomes. Just check the going rate for rentals in the new housing in your area.

Many older persons are being displaced from their present neighborhoods. A rental unit may be converted to a multiunit or a condominium. Or the original unit may be torn down and replaced with a more profitable commercial building or more expensive housing units. Housing for older persons is a critical

59

challenge for communities that is being met in a variety of ways.

"Aging in Place"

Fortunately, at least 75 percent of retirement-age persons own their own homes. *Shelter* for them means staying where they are. Much of this chapter is concerned with the 25 percent who require other options.

Nevertheless, the majority of older persons who own their homes face special problems. As persons become older and frailer, they need help in maintaining and repairing their homes. They may require minor remodeling such as installing ramps at doorways or grab bars in bathrooms. They need persons to help with cleanup chores or to provide transportation for shopping or visits to doctors and dentists. A neighborhood survey will identify such needs. And in Chapter 9 we talk about how many communities are responding to these kinds of needs.

The economic realities of home ownership for the elderly also require community awareness and help. When you live on a fixed income, tax increases threaten financial security. Taxes in most metropolitan areas have doubled and even tripled within the past decade, and homestead exemptions no longer provide a measure of relief. Older homeowners may prefer to remain in their mortgage-free residences but, because of inflation, can no longer do so.

Communities are helping older people to remain in their own homes with new imaginative financial programs.

Equity Conversion

Taxes get higher because assessed value of a residence is increased. Thus, equity (the actual current value of a property) is a valuable asset which is being tapped in a few experimental programs. One plan is called a Reverse Annuity Mortgage (RAM) Program and was developed by a nonprofit corporation, directed by a group of San Francisco civic leaders, in association with local banks.

The plan is based on a "sale and leaseback" arrangement, long used by businessmen wanting to keep cash flow as high as possible. In return for selling their homes at below-market prices, the elderly sellers are guaranteed the right of residency in their own homes for as long as they live. In addition, they receive a lifetime monthly income. They no longer have to pay taxes or insurance, nor are they burdened with major maintenance costs. They do pay a monthly rent.

This arrangement was tried in Marin County, California. A private pension fund invested nearly $1 million to purchase six properties, which had a market value of $1.2 million. The average discounted sale price of each home was $162,000. Each homeowner received a cash downpayment and will receive a monthly installment payment for the next ten to fifteen years. These monthly payments average $1,000 a month, from which the average rent of some $700 is deducted. A deferred annuity plan was purchased for each owner, so that the same monthly income is guaranteed beyond the installment period, should this be needed.

Conventional mortgages allow a person to live in a house while paying for it. *Equity conversion* plans enable a person to live in a house while selling it.

For more information, write:

National Center for Home Equity Conversion, 110 E. Main, Madison, WI 53703.

San Francisco Development Fund, RAM Program, 1107 Oak St., San Francisco, CA 94117.

Shared Housing

Once the financial pressures of retaining one's home are relieved, as in the equity conversion just described, the older homeowner may still require help in order to retain independence.

The term *frail elderly* is appearing frequently in geriatric literature. It simply recognizes that as persons age, they are unable to manage their lives as easily as in earlier years. They are weaker.

They develop certain disabilities, but these are rarely sufficiently severe to require institutionalization.

Sometimes these older persons are in actual danger. An eighty-nine-year-old blind woman, who owned her home, was abused by her brother-in-law; but now, with community help, she is still able to live independently. It makes great good sense to help people remain in their own homes as long as this is safely possible.

Shared housing is a way to achieve this goal. Here's how it works.

Let's assume that a single elderly homeowner (or renter) has a two- or three-bedroom house. Someone is found to share that home or apartment. That "someone" may be a retired couple, a student, another single elderly person, perhaps even a mentally retarded or partially disabled person. The blind lady mentioned earlier now has two low-income handicapped persons living with her. The arrangement is a kind of barter, or tradeoff. The person agreeing to share housing agrees to do certain things: perhaps it is eating one meal a day with the homeowner, mowing the lawn or raking leaves, vacuuming and dusting once a week, or being available as needed to take the homeowner to the doctor or to the supermarket for shopping. In exchange, the person gets a room and use of the kitchen. There could be some sharing of expenses, but if this is ever considered "rent," it could affect a future capital gains exemption allowed by the IRS when the house is sold (Congress is considering a bill to protect this exemption).

The matching-up of homeowner and companion is essential and critical, of course. This requires a local group to organize the program, to screen both homeowners and potential companions, to determine likes and dislikes for compatibility, and to facilitate and monitor the arrangement. Fortunately, excellent resources are available to any community wishing to explore this opportunity. More than three hundred such groups are already in existence.

For more information, including printed guides, planning materials, and workshop leadership, write: Shared Housing Resource Center, Inc., 6344 Greene St., Philadelphia, PA 19144.

For the experiences of Metropolitan Inter-Faith Association, one of the several hundred functioning groups, write: MIFA, P.O. Box 3130, Memphis, TN 38173. A similar group is Project MATCH, Inc., 277 W. Hedding St., San Jose, CA 95110.

Extended Housing

Among the many picturesque aspects of life in northern Indiana, which we enjoyed several years ago, were the irregular-shaped, frame Amish farmhouses. The strange profiles were due to the extra rooms, which were added on through the years as needed. Most often grandparents, the original builders, moved into the addition, while their children and grandchildren took over the "big house." This kind of extended family housing is part of fading Americana. Perhaps duplexes or triplexes may, one day, serve this kind of purpose, but I don't know of any current examples.

Australia has developed what it calls *granny flats*. These are small mobile prefab units, placed in the backyard owned by the family. The unit is rented to an older family member as long as needed; and then is moved to some other location, where it can again be used.

The term *granny flat* hasn't won much acceptance elsewhere, but there is something comparable in the United States called *ECHO Housing* (Elder Cottage Housing Opportunity). It is described as a housing arrangement that offers the older person an opportunity to live in close proximity to those who can help maintain the older person's independence and privacy. Also, such housing provides continuity of neighborhood, with familiar shopping areas, churches, and even bus stops. Experimental ECHO units may be found in several areas of the United States: Lancaster County, Pennsylvania; Arcata, Hemet, and Butte county, California; Rockville, Maryland; Tucson, Arizona; and Fairfax County, Virginia.

Most units are about the size of a two-car garage (504 square feet). Each unit has a living room, bedroom, bath, kitchen, pantry, and utility nook. Appliances include a stacked washer-dryer.

Some of the California units are as small as 280 square feet. Each unit is placed on a treated timber or cement block foundation, thus making it transportable at some future time. It is erected adjacent to a family dwelling, usually in the backyard. Cost ranges from $14,000 to $50,000.

Where local zoning regulations allow for such temporary structures, older homeowners will rent their larger home to others and live in ECHO housing. The extra income obviously helps. Renters are usually not family members. (Surprisingly, recent surveys indicate that parents have no great desire to live in proximity to their children. The converse may also be true.)

Communities interested in ECHO housing should first of all determine if such housing is permitted under current zoning regulations. Often it is forbidden, along with restrictions against mobile homes within city limits. While ECHO housing is "manufactured housing," it provides comfort and architectural compatibility not achievable with mobile housing. Nevertheless, if ECHO housing is not presently allowed in your city, a first step would be to secure such authorization.

For more information, write: Housing Program, American Association of Retired Persons, 1909 K. St. NW, Washington, DC 20049, and request the booklet *Echo Housing*. It contains a review of zoning issues and includes samples of enabling legislation.

Congregate Housing

This type of facility is usually a converted apartment house or apartment hotel. It is designed for older persons who are able to live independently but prefer the security and convenience of congregate living with persons their own age.

My mother, Anna, lived eighteen months in just such an environment. Initially she lived in The Governors, a former student dormitory adjacent to the University of Texas campus in Austin. It was managed by the Roman Catholic Diocese of Austin, which rented the facility. The diocese later purchased The Whitestone, a three-story conference center with sleeping quarters, in the same neighborhood, then sold the property back to its former manager, Floyd Martine.

The Whitestone is built on concrete piers, which allows for covered parking. An elevator serves the three floors. Rooms, located on all three levels, are built in clusters of three, with a small common lounge in each suite and two shower/commode units. There is room for 140 persons. The building is U-shaped and former conference rooms are located in the center. A large lounge with fireplace is on the first level, with a craft room and chapel nearby. The lounge opens out to an uncovered patio. The cafeteria is located on the second level.

Floyd Martine believes that "home" is still best for persons as long as this is possible and practical. He also feels there is a place for a facility halfway between independent home life and the nursing home. That's the purpose of The Whitestone.

All residents must be ambulatory. There is no nursing staff since this is not a nursing home; staff is not permitted to administer medications. Eighty percent of the residents are women; 20 percent are men. Rooms and suites are cleaned once a week. Residents arrange for their own laundry; coin-operated washers and dryers are located on two levels. Three hot meals are served daily, and juice and hot beverages are available throughout the day. Martine provides this kind of environment for $500 a month, which includes room and board. He is proud of the fact that he operates without any government funding.

The facility lacks a social worker but does have a chaplain, who has stayed on from the diocesan days. Churches and campus Greek-letter societies provide activities and entertainment. Student nurses conduct two health workshops each year. The house manager frequently buses tables in order to be in closer contact with the residents.

Street doors are locked at 9 P.M. Residents are free to come and go but must "check out" if they plan to stay elsewhere overnight. There are no bed-checks but breakfast tables are monitored; this is a practical way to determine who may have wandered off or may be ill. Martine says few residents ever voluntarily miss breakfast.

Floyd Martine believes there should be many more such facilities. He thinks they can survive more easily in cities of a hundred thousand or more. He likes the idea of suites because there is value in a grouping of two or three people who look after each other. Each person, however, should have his or her own private room. And he would prefer a separate shower and commode for each resident. He insists upon showers, convinced that they are safer than baths. (I wonder whether a single bath on each level, with appropriate safety features such as grab bars, would help those persons who occasionally like to soak, and could benefit from it.)

Martine wishes he had more storage space for residents' items. And he admits that it is easier to cope with emerging physical handicaps but much more difficult to deal with persons with increasing confusion and disorientation. He would like to have a full-time social worker to help his residents and their families.

Martine operates a clean, hospitable facility. While it is a commercial venture, it realizes only a very small profit because of its low monthly fees. Other entrepreneurs with a dedicated sense of public service could do likewise. Another example is Saint Leonard's Center for the Elderly in Centerville, Ohio (near Dayton), which was the campus of the Franciscan Seminary until 1981.

Older hotels and apartment houses could be salvaged to good purpose, rather than sacrificed to inner city urban development. Nonprofit groups may be able to secure government loans for converting older structures into special housing for senior adults under Section 202 of the National Housing Act (which is described in more detail in the following section). Any group, profit or nonprofit, might obtain federal funding under Section 234 of that same Act. Check with your nearest HUD office for more information (see Appendix D for addresses).

For more information about The Whitestone operation, write: Floyd Martine, 2819 Rio Grande, Austin, TX 78705.

Retirement Residences

These are private residences, usually apartments, designed for older persons who have both will and health to live independently but choose to do so in a communal, supportive setting. Many nonprofit groups have sponsored such retirement residence projects with substantial government assistance.

Village Christian Apartments
Austin, Texas

This project, sponsored by the Brentwood Church of Christ, began with an idea in 1969. It took ten years of study, planning, and negotiating with HUD (the U.S. Department of Housing and Urban Development) before it opened in January, 1979.

Its present population is 113, of which only ten are men. You must be sixty-two years old to be eligible to apply. Nevertheless, the average age of people who have entered the facility was eighty. Two-thirds of those original tenants are still living in Village Christian Apartments, and they are now in their nineties.

This has several ramifications. First, many elderly people have been able to manage independently, thereby avoiding institutionalization. Second, the population is older and frailer, and some of the original recreational programs no longer have the participation they once did (not many people manage outdoor gardening anymore, for example). Third, there are very few vacancies. In fact, there is a waiting list of more than three hundred people for one of the 105 apartments. Average waiting time is three-and-a-half years.

Six of its all-electric apartments have two bedrooms, ninety-five have one bedroom, and four are efficiencies. Ten apartments have been modified for handicapped persons, with wider doors for wheelchairs, grab bars, lowered light switches, total ceramics in bathrooms, and openings under sink and counters for wheelchair accessibility. The lovely apartment complex is located near two shopping malls, a supermarket, and a four-screen theatre. There is plenty of lighted parking.

There are two U-shaped buildings facing each other, with

three levels and elevators in each building. A landscaped patio is in the center. Ground level contains offices, a huge lounge area with fireplace, a library, a craft room, a store, post office, and a beauty shop. Garden plots, with water taps, are located in back of the building.

There is also a dining area, used for occasional meals, and a kitchen. The kitchen is used primarily to prepare meals to be delivered in the Meals on Wheels program. Many residents actively participate in this program.

Staff consists of a manager, an activities coordinator, and a newly employed counselor. Support staff includes secretarial, security, and maintenance help. The staff meets twice a month to review specific relationships and problems of residents. Dessie Lee Honeycutt, the manager, told me that families are very much involved with the lives and needs of their relatives who are residents. Most of the families are from surrounding central Texas, and Mrs. Honeycutt believes that the frontier sense of the *family* and *family reunions* is still very strong.

The counselor says most of her work is trying to help residents face grief and fear. An emerging need is to help residents face future reality, when their independence may no longer be possible.

Meanwhile, three out of ten residents exhibit their independence at every opportunity. The facility owns a van and it is used frequently. Residents who choose to do so eat out together once a week, usually for breakfast. They go shopping together and attend the annual circus. Twice a year in spring and fall, they travel seventy miles to LBJ Ranch, the "Texas Whitehouse" of President Lyndon Baines Johnson. (The spring trip features acres of blooming bluebonnets and other wildflowers for which central Texas is so famous.) Birthday parties are held monthly. Bible classes and bingo games are held weekly.

There is no entrance fee but rent must be paid. Your annual income cannot exceed $15,850 if you are single or $18,300 if you are married. No minimum income is required. Rental is set by HUD at 30 percent of your income. Thus, if you are married and have an annual income of $18,000, your monthly rent will be one-twelfth of $6,000, or $500 per month. Utilities are individually metered and are extra.

For more information, write: Village Christian Apartments, 7925 Rockwood Lane, Austin, TX 78758.

Trinity Place Apartments
Round Rock, Texas

This sixty-eight-unit facility, which is also a HUD 202 project, opened in late 1984 and is operated by Lutheran Social Service of Texas. It required three years of planning and negotiation. Round Rock is a growing suburb of Austin, and Trinity Place is located on the south edge of the city, next door to an elementary school and two blocks from a large shopping center.

Trinity Place Apartments are either one-bedroom or efficiency units. Ten of these are designed for handicapped use. In addition to wider doors and grab bars, they also feature handheld showers and no overhead cabinets. An emergency response lifeline system is provided, connected with Trinity Lutheran Nursing Home, located some three miles away. All units are built at ground level. Norman Hein, director of the project, believes that "earth is part of the Texas lifestyle." Thus, residents may have a garden, if they wish, in their backyard, as well as a place to hang out the clothes.

There is a laundromat on the grounds, as well as a community center, a kitchen, and a secure post box area. The city is building sidewalks, with federal block grant funding. As is the case with Village Christian Apartments, applicants must be sixty-two years old or older and meet the identical income requirements.

I was curious as to why Village Christian Apartments had so few two-bedroom units, and Trinity Place had none. It seems to me that an extra bedroom would be helpful when a resident requires a live-in companion or a nurses' aide. (HUD regulations do not allow two persons of the same sex to share the same bedroom.) Norman Hein told me it is a question of economics. Adding an extra bedroom adds $10,000 to construction costs per unit, and federal money, while still available, is given in smaller amounts and with more restrictions.

For more information about Trinity Place, write: Lutheran Social Service of Texas, P.O. Box 49589, Austin, TX 78765-9589.

Cypen Tower
Douglas Gardens, Miami, Florida

Cypen Tower is an eight-story apartment building located on the grounds of the Miami Jewish Home and Hospital for the Aged. It contains 102 studio and one-bedroom apartments. It is unique for several reasons.

The building cost $3.3 million and received no federal funding, since it was financed entirely through private contributions. Thus, Cypen Tower has no mortgage and no debt service costs. Also, rentals (ranging from $574 to $692) are set to cover operating costs only and include a daily hot meal. The facility is thus able to admit a middle-income person whose resources may be just *above* the guidelines established by federal agencies.

The building was planned with suggestions from future residents. Interior design was done by senior students of Miami-area professional schools. The architects had experience in designing health-care facilities and incorporated such things as a five-foot turning radius in bathrooms and kitchens and short pile carpeting. All apartments have bathtubs with a built-in tile bench. An emergency call system is available to all, as is a built-in TV cable system over which special programs and films are transmitted within the building.

For more information, write: Cypen Tower, Douglas Gardens, Miami Jewish Home and Hospital for the Aged, 151 NE 52d St., Miami, FL 33137.

Cooperative Housing

One other arrangement for residential housing should be mentioned. Cooperative Services, Inc. (CSI), is a three-thousand member consumer cooperative with a forty-year history. It began as a co-op dairy, with depots that distributed milk to members at cost. Today, it is the largest senior-citizen housing cooperative in the United States. Its first cooperative apartment building was a 139-unit complex built in 1959 in Wyandotte, Michigan. Today, it manages ten independent housing projects of 150 to 250 units each, and has plans for several more in California,

Maryland, Massachusetts, and Michigan. It has benefited from HUD funding.

These are not condominiums, in which residents own their individual apartments. Rather, as a consumer co-op, residents are consumer-owners but do not hold any individual equity interest. A member pays a one-time $100 membership fee (unchanged since the 1940s) which is returned if the member withdraws from CSI. Each member has an equal vote in electing the board of directors. A seventy-member "Cooperative Congress" meets three times a year to review the performance of its board. The apartment buildings are managed by volunteer residents through an elected council. The only full-time paid employee in each building is the custodian. Rentals are the ones established by HUD, but savings realized by cooperative management provide a healthy reserve for maintenance and earlier repayment of loans.

For more information, write: Cooperative Services, Inc., 740 Woodward, Detroit, MI 48226.

Retirement Communities

These are similar to retirement residences, but are towns, villages, or subdivisions usually made up of individual dwellings. The communities offer shopping facilities, a post office, churches, and community activities.

Examples: Bristol Village, Waverly, Ohio, and the former Aldersgate Community near Kissimmee, Florida. One of the newest older communities in Arizona is Green Valley, located south of Tucson. Such projects require major capitalization but offer special challenges to architects and developers. HUD loans may be available through Title VII (1970) and Title IV (1968) programs.

Condominiums

This is the story of several older couples who sold their residences, pooled their resources, and built an eighteen-apartment complex of their own design. They did it without federal funding but had to take on City Hall before they were finished. The result is called *Heritage Square*, owned by the Lawnmont Heritage Square Homeowners Association of Austin, Texas.

The units are built on a one-and-a-quarter acre site in north Austin. Two senior citizen housing projects are close-by, one operated by the city, the other by a health-care organization. A shopping center with supermarket and cafeteria is two blocks away. Also close-by is a public library, a city bus line, and even a fantastic ice cream parlor called Udder Delight. It is an excellent location for older people.

The one-and-a-quarter acre site presented problems, however. The parcel of land was made up of two lots; one of these was zoned for single dwellings. To get something rezoned for multidwellings requires the consent of the majority (more than 50 percent) of the neighbors. This took time but once achieved there was the problem of securing rain drains and both water and sewer hookups. The mayor finally intervened with the city's utility and public works departments. It took four years to get the necessary clearances, which is a long time for people past sixty-five to wait and hope for new housing.

They occupied their architect-designed, eighteen-unit brick complex in early 1982. Half of the units are at ground level, facing the street. The rest are in a two-story building, in the rear, with an elevator. There is covered parking. Each unit averages twelve hundred square feet. A sprinkling system was installed to water the lawn. Neighbors objected to floodlights, but walkway lights and a privacy fence on three sides provide a measure of security.

How did eighteen people ever get together on such a project? Herschel Gipson was the catalyst. He knew that a parcel of land was for sale, and he talked up the project at his church and a local senior citizens center. People simply responded; several did not know each other before the project began. There are former pharmacists, teachers, professors, a lawyer, businesspeople, and secretaries. One resident still commutes to work. The majority of the residents are widows. Only four men live in the complex.

Decisions are made by a five-member board. Two new members are elected each year. This system of rotation provides both continuity and fresh input.

Bob Barkley is the current spokesman and treasurer of the association. He is reasonably happy with their achievement. Financially, it has worked out well. Owners pay their own taxes (all can claim a homestead exemption which reduces taxes) and utilities. Each owner pays $50 a month as a maintenance fee. This covers water and mowing of the lawn. Bob thinks that monthly amount may have to be increased to build up a reserve to replace the roof one of these days. There is no mortgage. Each resident owns his or her apartment which can be sold or, at the time of death, becomes part of that person's estate.

What Bob doesn't particularly like is the lack of storage space (which I found to be a common complaint in every type of housing for the elderly!). "Older people have too much stuff," he says, "and you never get rid of as much as you should."

I was curious about socialization. There is no clubhouse or swimming pool, for example. I was surprised to learn that so few of the residents bother to share a meal together in the cafeteria located just across the street.

Bob Barkley explained that the residents have gotten older and frailer. But he insists there is a sense of community. If someone is sick, a neighbor brings food. If someone needs to get to a doctor, someone provides transportation. But they don't visit each other much. They don't often attend church anymore. And Bob thinks they are happy with their situation, content to have comfortable shelter and to be financially secure.

Bob Barkley would do it again. He recommends that (1) you bring together a compatible group, one that gets along with each other, (2) you have a group that brings with it a variety of experience (this helps the group to face and solve new problems), and (3) you begin with a good, solid plan and an organization.

The condominium idea is not new, of course. What is different about Heritage Square is that it was designed and developed by senior citizens themselves. If you would like more information, write Bob Barkley at Heritage Square No. 10, 2301 Lawnmont, Austin, TX 78756.

Lutheran Social Service of Texas has developed its own version of the condominium. It is located in Edna, forty miles from the Gulf Coast, and consists of duplexes. Apartments are relatively large—from nine to twelve hundred square feet. The facility was privately financed and a "lifetime lease" requires a payment of between $40,000 to $50,000. The monthly maintenance fee ranges from $100 to $150. No meals are provided since the city of Edna has an active senior center where meals are served.

The financing arrangement differs from other facilities: if a resident decides to move, a substantial portion of the entrance fee is returned to the resident (or to the estate, in case of death). After five years, it is 50 percent of what was paid (which is the maximum thereafter). An extra 5 percent is added for each year prior to the five-year period (if a person left after three years, for example, he or she would receive 65 percent of the entrance fee). Since federal funding is not involved, there are no restrictions on residency, other than the ability to pay.

For information about the Edna project, write: Lutheran Social Service of Texas, P.O. Box 49589, Austin, TX 78765-9589.

Lifecare Facilities

Lifecare means just that: a facility that provides both shelter and long-term health care, if needed. The facility might be a retirement village or a high-rise apartment unit, but the facility will include a nursing home and/or hospital. Costs are high and usually require a substantial "endowment" payment upon entry, plus a monthly fee.

Trinity Towers, which opened its doors in early 1985 in Corpus Christi, Texas, is a fairly typical example of this kind of facility.

It has nineteen stories and 204 units, each having some view of Corpus Christi Bay. The building includes a thirty-bed nursing facility. There is a dining room, a library, barber-beauty shop, free washer and dryer on each floor, an outdoor swimming pool, and other amenities.

The entrance fee ranges from $30,000 to $95,000. The resident does not purchase the apartment, but only *life occupancy* with guarantee of permanent nursing care, if needed. Under this plan, nothing is returned to the resident or his/her estate. Trinity Towers publicity states that a portion of the lifecare entrance fee, estimated at 17 percent, may be deductible as a medical expense in the year paid. It refers to IRS ruling 76-481, but this should be confirmed with a tax consultant.

For an additional 25 percent a resident signs up for a *refundable estate* plan. The resident enjoys all privileges except getting credit for a bed in the nursing facility. Thus, lifecare is not part of the contract. However, 95 percent of the entrance fee is refundable if the resident leaves or dies.

There are monthly fees which range from $655 to $1,525. These include twice-a-month housekeeping, weekly flat laundry service, payment of all utilities, and one meal a day. Transportation for shopping or to churches is provided. Jody Lamping, director of resident relations, says candidly that "it takes someone who is not indigent to participate here. Trinity Towers was designed particularly for middle and upper-middle income people, because the government and the churches do take care of the poor. There's nobody to take care of this class of people."

Nevertheless, Trinity Towers was begun by two Corpus Christi churches: First Presbyterian and the Episcopal Church of the Good Shepherd. A broadly based board now governs Whole Life, Incorporated, which owns the facility. Its major task was to secure funding, achieved through $28.9 million of industrial revenue bonds, approved by the Corpus Christi city council. No federal or other public funding is involved.

The facility is managed by the Hospital Building and Equipment Company of Saint Louis.

Laventhol and Horwath, a national public accounting and consulting company, says there are some six hundred lifecare communities in operation in the United States. They predict that at least another one thousand will be established by 1990 to meet the needs of elderly persons in the middle and upper-middle income brackets.

For more information, write:

Trinity Towers of Coastal Bend, 3747 S. Alameda, Corpus Christi, TX 78411.

HBE Corporation, P.O. Box 27339, Saint Louis, MO 63141.

Nursing Homes

Less than 5 percent of elderly persons live in nursing homes at any given time, but it is estimated that 20 percent of older persons will eventually enter a long-term health facility. Such persons have an average age of eighty-four. Nursing homes provide continuing care at two levels: *intermediate* care for persons who need help with the routines of living and *skilled* care for those who require constant nursing care. There is a need for well-administered, caring, and competent long-term health facilities.

Civic and church consortia may want to explore ownership and management possibilities. Existing facilities might be purchased. New "state-of-the-healing-art" nursing homes could be built. HUD insures mortgages to finance construction or renovation of facilities under Section 232 (National Housing Act, 1934) and Section 115 (Housing Act, 1959). Consult HUD field offices for specific information.

For additional information, write:

American Association of Homes for the Aging, 1050 17th St. NW, Suite No. 770, Washington, DC 20036 (this is the trade group for nonprofit groups).

American Health Care Association, 1200 15th St. NW, Washington, DC 20005 (the trade group for commercial operators).

With a Little Help from Our Friends

Here are a few ideas from other countries about housing for older persons.

Japan provides low-interest loans to families wishing to add a room to their home to accommodate an elderly relative.

Sweden builds "service houses" for older adults in an integrated setting. Apartments for healthy persons are linked by an alarm system to a central location in case of any emergency. Apartments for the frail elderly are designed to facilitate their activity. Home care and delivered meals are available. The Goteborg service house includes a floor for respite care, admitting older persons on a short-term basis while their families are ill or away on vacation. In the city of Lidingo, the complex includes facilities which are used by the entire community: a center, a sports pavilion, a public library, a nursery and elementary school, and art studios. A covered walkway joins the development to the local hospital.

France provides a vacation home for the elderly in the Vosges mountain region, used both in summer and winter.

Great Britain has a "gifted house program," in which older persons owning houses too large for their needs donate them to a charity organization ("Help the Aged"). That organization then remodels the house into several apartments, returning one of the redesigned flats to the former owner rent-free for the rest of his or her life, or that of the surviving spouse. Remodeled houses include central heating and safety features. The former owner is relieved of all taxes and maintenance expense. Sharing the house with others increases opportunities for companionship and help in emergencies.

HUD

Finally, let's take a look at federal funding for some of these projects. The legal authority is Section 202 of the Housing Act of 1959 (P.L. 86-372), which is administered by the Department of Housing and Urban Development. The shortened name is *HUD 202* housing.

The purpose of the law is to "provide housing and related facilities for the elderly and the handicapped." It provides long-term *loans* (not grants) to eligible private nonprofit sponsors to finance rental or cooperative housing facilities for elderly or handicapped persons. The government charges interest, which is variable (Trinity Place is paying 9 1/4 percent).

Rents are established at "fair market" levels and residents pay up to 30 percent of their income as rent. If that amount does not meet local fair market rentals, then the government subsidizes rents up to that level (this is done under authority of Section 8, U.S. Housing Act of 1937, P.L. 730479, as added by the Housing and Community Act of 1974, P.L. 93-383). It may appear to be robbing a government Peter to pay a government Paul, but HUD, nevertheless, will get its money. If the nonprofit management fails to meet its payments, HUD will foreclose. However, when the forty-year loan is paid, the nonprofit sponsors will own the facility.

The HUD 202 loan is a *100* percent loan. Thus, there is a scramble to secure this kind of funding and applicants need considerable help not only to compete, but also to work their way through the maze of bureaucratic jargon and regulations.

Pastor Norman Hein, a former nursing home administrator, an MSW who once worked for the state welfare department, explained the process Lutheran Social Service followed in developing Trinity Place. The first thing any potential developer must do, he says, is to employ a consultant who has previously worked on HUD 202 projects. Later, you will need a lawyer, unless your consultant is also a lawyer. Upon request, HUD will provide listings of consultants. Also, a developer should check with other groups who have already gone through this process and ask for their recommendations.

Lutheran Social Service budgeted $20,000 to get started. This was needed for land commitments, architectural designs, and required incorporation costs. This is up-front, risk money. If you get your loan, you may get some of this money returned to you. If you don't get your loan, you've spent some money on experience and education.

The required documentation is formidable. The original application of Trinity Place fills a two-inch thick notebook, containing twenty-five separate exhibits and five appendices. These include descriptions of proposed housing, anticipated occupancy, evidence of the borrower's local community base, evidence of the borrower's capability to sponsor, develop, own, manage, and provide special services—as well as the many required forms. After Lutheran Social Service of Texas received preliminary favorable response to its application, Trinity Place was then required to submit additional information related to a "conditional commitment." Much of this was of technical nature, but this second submission included another twenty-eight exhibits!

So, to reiterate, don't begin this process without a consultant. Norm Hein says, "Only the persistent get through."

To be fair, HUD isn't merely concerned with paper work. Since it distributes large sums of taxpayers' money, it carefully screens all applicants. But once you have satisfied the requirements, HUD is there to help you. In fact, it helps you before you begin by conducting preapplication conferences. By now you have a consultant, a lawyer, and an architect. Once your application is approved, you will hire a contractor. HUD holds monthly preconstruction conferences with architect, contractor, and developer. There are also sessions dealing with preoccupancy, pre-opening, and post-opening. Behind this jargon is the fact that this particular government agency wants you to succeed.

Norman Hein has one other suggestion. The three rules of getting started, he says, are "site, site, and site." He means that accessible location is paramount, not only for securing a government loan, but also for the ultimate success of the venture. A clear title is essential.

Such projects are not for the faint-hearted, but if you are blessed with stamina and qualified, supportive colleagues, something truly significant in housing for the elderly can be accomplished. And the projects survive. There is a San Antonio program known as the West Durango Plaza Apartments, begun in 1967, whose eighty-two units are filled, mostly with elderly people. The complex is well maintained and the El Divino Redentor Presbyterian Church, the Hispanic congregation which started the project, will own it in the year 2007.

The examples thus far are all church-related. However, churches are by no means the only sponsors of HUD 202 housing. Any nonprofit organization may apply. One example is the American Legion, which built a sixty-unit project on twelve acres of land in Hanover, Massachusetts. It is pictured in the December

1982 issue of the *AIA Journal* (trade journal of the American Institute of Architects). It consists of three clusters of twenty units. All face a central courtyard and the bedrooms overlook the surrounding woods. Each apartment has two exposures for natural ventilation. There is one apartment designed for disabled persons in each of the three clusters.

If you are interested in pursuing this kind of project, get in touch with your nearest HUD area office as soon as possible. There are deadlines for submitting applications and there are always new regulations and procedures with which to become familiar. A list of HUD addresses appears in Appendix D.

Practical Design Considerations

When you build, build the very best and appropriate facility that you can. Secure expert help in design, not only from architects but also from interior designers who understand the needs of handicapped persons.

Door handles are preferable to door knobs, for example. Three-foot-wide doors are best and doors should not be installed flush to any wall. A one-foot minimum is required on the pull side of the door to permit a person using a wheelchair or walking aid to move close to the handle of the door, pull it open, and then go through the doorway. Walls should be reinforced for grab bars. Light switches should be lowered. Ramps and other barrier-free access should be planned before construction begins.

Interior decorators can help design kitchen and other work areas for persons in wheelchairs. Kitchen cabinets can be built with turntable shelves. Stoves should have controls in front of the unit. Access below sinks and counters is needed. A Dutch firm (Medinorm [R] Holland, P.O. Box 137, 9400 AC Assen, The Netherlands) specializes in *ergonomical* kitchens, which feature adjustments for handicapped or small people. However, standard equipment and cabinetry can be adapted.

Resources

For the serious planner of housing, I recommend the book *Housing For The Elderly* by Rosetta E. Parker. This is a handbook for managers but contains helpful general information as well as specifics for professionals. It is published by the Institute of Real Estate Management, 430 N. Michigan Ave., Chicago, IL 60611-4090. It is an expensive, large-format paperback (about $20) but well worth the price.

Another paperback (and much more expensive, about $75) is the book *How To Get Government Loans* by Wayne Phillips. It is intended for real estate investors and entrepreneurs, but does include descriptions of dozens of government programs with samples of forms. Publisher is Impact Publishing Co., 2110 Omega Rd., Suite A, San Ramon, CA 94583. Perhaps you could borrow a copy from your friendly realtor.

And Dr. Paul Maves has written a helpful volume, *A Place to Live in Your Later Years*, with Augsburg publishers. This is a good discussion guide for anyone who wants to take a serious look at living/housing options for the elderly.

There exists an extremely great need for housing for older persons. This very long chapter gives evidence that there are many solutions. If the survey of your community indicates that housing is the priority need of your older neighbors, then you and your study group may want to review this chapter again, taking note of the approaches you would like to explore further with administrators of similar programs and other housing experts.

6

Daytime Shelter
Day Care Centers for Adults

It is estimated that at least 30 percent, and perhaps as many as half, of the residents in nursing homes don't really require long-term health care. With a little bit of help and monitoring, they could live out their lives (or delay around-the-clock nursing home care) at less public expense in a private home. Many children care for their parents or other loved ones in their homes; Carolyn and I were among them. Others live in foster homes.

We are talking about the special category of older persons described in current gerontological literature as the "frail elderly," the "substantially homebound," or persons with "accumulated handicaps." They are not the chronically ill nor severely disabled.

This "little bit of help and monitoring" often becomes a gigantic and unwieldy effort for family caregivers, since it means that another adult needs to be close-by and available to the patient. That other adult doesn't have to be a nurse, at least if only oral medication is required. And medication may not even be required. The frail older person may merely be confused and tend to wander; he or she may be physically weak and need assistance to the restroom or help at mealtime.

We hired paraprofessional medical aides to help us care for Carolyn's dad, Paul Young. That meant having one full-time or two part-time persons work a total of 40 to 50 hours a week, which still left 128 or 118 hours each week for us to fill. We did this at two separate times, during our seven-year care of Paul. (He was in a nursing home the rest of that time.)

Paul's resources and ours, limited as they were, allowed us to do this for a time. But what if the caregiver works for minimum wage or is on welfare? Most caregivers are women and many of them, especially from low-income minority groups, earn their living as waitresses or service persons. Their schedules are erratic. They cannot afford hired caregivers.

Too often, then, the only perceivable solution seems to be a nursing home. The family member simply isn't able to or can't afford to care for a frail parent at home. Since the family member likely falls below the federal poverty guideline (which in 1984 was an annual income of $4,980 for an individual), federal and state assistance becomes available to pay for the much more expensive nursing home care. Similar assistance is not available in all states for chore care or companion care in the home, and where it is available, funds are minimal. Thus, nursing home populations increase.

There is another solution, and it is the *adult day care center*. Unfortunately, there are still too few of them—less than nine hundred in the entire United States (less than twenty in the state of Texas).

Day care centers should not be confused with senior centers (discussed in Chapter 4), although they may sometimes be related to them. Senior centers provide socialization and stimulation for ambulatory, healthy older persons. There are some nine thousand of them. A tenth of that number are adult day care centers.

Adult day care is a generic term that applies to a variety of programs and services. You will see categories such as day care, day treatment, day health care, psychiatric day treatment, partial hospitalization, and day hospital care. In fact, adult day care originated in hospitals, first in England (Cowley Road Hospital, Oxford, in 1950), and in North Carolina (Cherry State Hospital, Goldsboro, in 1960).

There was no rapid growth of other centers, however. Maryland and Arizona experimented with the concept in the 1970s, taking advantage of funding through Title III of the Older Americans Act. Title XIX (Medicaid) and Title XX funds (through the Social Security Act) encouraged further development in the later

1970s and early 1980s. But the idea is still fresh and largely untried.

The qualifying word in *adult day care* is "care." Such centers provide the help and monitoring that are essential for elderly persons whose functional levels are impaired. Abilities are encouraged and developed. Helen Padula, formerly with the Maryland Department of Health and Mental Hygiene, defines *day care* as "one of many services intended to help impaired adults and their families or other caregivers keep going a little longer."

Carol H. Kurland of the New Jersey Division of Medical Assistance and Health Services says that "medical day care can be the way station or transitional stage for some participants moving into nursing homes—or rehabilitative for others who need protective care for an acute period and can move to a less dependent social setting or back to their own homes after a temporary period of care."

The Maryland Department of Health and Mental Hygiene developed its definition of *day care* in 1970:

> Day care... means any program which provides personal care, supervision, and an organized program of activities, experiences, and therapies during the day in a protective group setting. Day care offers an individualized plan of care designed to maintain impaired persons at, or to restore them to, optimal capability of self-care.

The goal of day care is more than just providing custodial care—"keeping an eye on the old folks." In Denmark, goals are stated as *activate, motivate,* and *rehabilitate.* Others, in this country, talk about *maintenance* and objectives that are *social* (or *psychosocial*) and *restorative.*

Social emphasizes socialization for participants, while providing caregivers a regularly scheduled respite. This is a kind of extended, day-long senior center, with activities geared to the special needs of participants. *Maintenance* is a step beyond mere socialization; it seeks to maintain a level of awareness and mobility. This goal requires physical exercise, attention to nutrition, and reality orientation. *Restorative* refers to rehabilitation and remedial services that look forward to improvement or restoration of skills and abilities.

Staff-to-client ratios are at least one staff person for every eight clients. The recommended ratio is 1:5. A new Alzheimer's center on the West Coast has one staff person for every two participants. Staff members are *enablers*, helping frail elderly people to help themselves.

We had a five-month experience with adult day care in our caregiving to Paul Young. (He attended a senior center at an earlier stage.) We used the day care center two or three times a week, filling in the other days with an aide in our home. This is not an unusual pattern; few participants in adult day care programs attend every day.

The program was started by two women, one a registered nurse, the other a professional social worker. They called their center, a six-room frame house centrally located in Austin, Hearts Inc. The building had formerly been used as a massage parlor, which produced some interesting and colorful exchanges as former clients occasionally returned, only to find a different ownership and operation.

There were singing, crafts, outdoor walking excursions, a hot lunch, an area for after-lunch napping, acupressure treatments (using the principle of acupuncture but with massage and pressure), and discussion and conversation. The charge was $16 a day, which did not include transportation. The ladies did not accept Medicaid patients, because they chose to avoid the licensing and paper work involved with any influx of federal money. They felt a program was needed for middle-income people, who could pay their own way.

They needed sixteen participants just to break even. Despite advertising and some helpful public relations in local media, they never had more than twelve. Their program failed for lack of public support, and the building is now used by a podiatrist.

Donna Loflin, a pioneer in the field of adult day care, says a group needs to allow two or even three years for the project to get off the ground. Too many programs fold after six months. Of the nineteen adult day care centers presently operating in Texas, only three are slightly above the break-even point. It isn't a way for an entrepreneur to make money.

Let's review a few programs that have some history and experience, programs that are "hanging in there" and hope to survive.

Austin Adult Day Care Centers

There are two centers, sponsored by Lutheran Social Service of Texas, functioning in Austin.

One is the East Austin Adult Day Care Center, which was started by Donna Loflin in 1977. Its first site was the basement of a Roman Catholic church in a predominantly Black and Hispanic part of the city. It now operates from a large frame house, which has been modified with ramps. Donna has left to begin another program called The Errand Service, Inc.

The East Side Center is licensed (by the Texas Departments of Human Resources and Health) for thirty persons. It has twenty-nine on its rolls. They suffer from hypertension, congestive heart failure, seizure, brain trauma, schizophrenia (but another diagnosis is required to remain in the center), and Alzheimer's disease (ranging from early stages to severe). The Alzheimer's people will probably be the first to be transferred to a nursing home.

Most clients live in the East Side. They have a low income and little education. Some live in foster homes. Four of the twenty-nine still live alone (they suffer from arthritis, mild hypertension, and early Alzheimer's). There is only one private-pay person. Besides their medical problems, clients need help with their finances, food stamp applications, and other matters requiring a counselor.

This particular center, however, is licensed as a medical unit and must have either a registered or a licensed practical nurse. Much time is taken with keeping doctor's orders (which must be reviewed by the doctor every six months), giving or supervising medication, taking blood pressure, and trying to get clients (and their families, if they are involved) to continue medical treatment over the weekends, when the center is closed. There is a large amount of government-generated paperwork, relating to funding and mandated training programs for personnel. This center is located in a poverty area, and each staff person has to cope with the personal frustration of working with clients and families who are often illiterate and unmotivated.

A typical day will include reality orientation, where a staff member provides gentle reminders about the time, date, place, upcoming holidays, and important new events. There are arts and crafts. Bible study is a favorite segment. There will be outings to a park, a flea market, or the governor's mansion. They play ring toss and bingo. Some members like to go to the kitchen to bake. There is music for singing and exercise—and occasional dancing.

Staff consists of a director-nurse, a social worker (who is also the activities director), one driver, two aides, one home aide, one janitor, and two volunteer workers. Some are trainees in city programs. It is difficult, debilitating work, and staff burn-out is the occupational hazard.

Regular meals are secured from the Senior Luncheon Program of the Parks and Recreation Department. Special diet meals are provided, at cost, from Holy Cross Hospital, whose dietician is on call and who reviews snack diets and personal dietary needs of clients.

The East Side Center, despite its twenty-nine participants, does not make any profit. In fact, it has an annual deficit in the neighborhood of $30,000, which must be made up through contributions or direct subsidy from its sponsoring Lutheran social agency.

The second Lutheran facility in Austin is the South Austin Adult Day Care Center. The Colorado River divides Austin between north and south; the southside center accepts clients from anywhere, but provides van transportation only to persons living south of the river.

The center is lodged in a small but attractive brick building in a public housing project. The building was formerly an office and a community center. This adult day care center is not licensed for medical care and has no resident registered or practical nurse, although a nurse or nursing trainee visits weekly to check blood pressure and monitor other health conditions.

The emphasis at this center is socialization and occupational therapy. The schedule is filled with many of the same components that the East Austin Center provides, although there seems to be more emphasis upon ADL (Activities of Daily Living), which is especially helpful to persons coping with memory loss.

The number of participants varies from month to month, but ranges between twenty-five and thirty. Daily attendance shifts from nine to seventeen. Daily fees are based upon a person's ability to pay, ranging from $8 to $20 per day. Staff consists of a director, a social worker, two part-time activities directors, and two drivers. There are usually two volunteers each day, who are often students from the University of Texas School of Social Work and School of Nursing.

Operating hours for both the east and southside centers are from 7:30 A.M. until 5:30 P.M., Monday through Friday.

However, the director of The South Austin Center, Debbie Williams, began an evening care program on Tuesdays and Thursdays, when the center stays open until 9 P.M. A soup-and-sandwich supper is provided on those evenings, and a staff activity coordinator is on duty. It is a great idea that provides some extra needed respite for caregivers, but thus far average attendance is only two or three persons per evening. The extra cost is $4.50 an hour.

For information about either center, write: Lutheran Social Service of Texas, Inc., P.O. Box 49589, Austin, TX 78765-9589.

Adult Day Care of Fort Worth

The Dallas-Fort Worth Metroplex is ranked as the eighth most populous area in the United States, based on the 1980 census (up from twelfth place in 1970). There is only one adult day care center in each of these major cities. We will take a look at the one in Fort Worth.

When I asked director Arlen Valdness how it is financed, he quickly replied, "The Lord!" He is reimbursed by the Texas Department of Human Resources, gets some assistance from the city, charges $20 a day for participants who can pay it, and receives some help from individual contributors and Saint Bartholomew's Roman Catholic Church, where he is a member. The annual budget is $60,000; there is no surplus.

There are forty clients, and average attendance varies from twenty to twenty-six.

The day I visited the center, there were three clusters of people. One group was discussing current events, as the volunteer leader went through selected parts of the daily newspaper. Another group was working on a puzzle and crafts. A third group was setting tables for lunch. There was a happy background buzz of chatter and occasional laughter. The center is open from 7 A.M. until 5 P.M.

Paid staff consists of the director, a social services director who doubles as an activities coordinator, an LVN (Licensed Vocational Nurse), an aide (sometimes there are two), and volunteers. I asked Valdness what volunteers do. "I work heck out of 'em!" he said. One is a driver, who himself lives in a foster home. Volunteers are involved in everything and anything—and are probably responsible for the relatively low budget for so large an operation.

The center has moved to a former elementary school building, about a mile from its previous location in an old Assembly of God church. The cafeteria wing is now used for the day care center. The auditorium wing houses the food bank and soup kitchen. Transportation is provided by two highboy vans with lifts and a station wagon.

Arlen Valdness is a former electrical contractor, aerospace engineer, and photographic scientist (who helped develop the Unicolor process). He and Mrs. Valdness searched "for something more significant to do in life." That decision led, first, to becoming an administrator of a retirement village and, since, to the adult day care ministry. They demonstrate what individuals can do when they have a vision and large reserves of energy.

The adult day care center is just one facet of this special ministry in Fort Worth. An adjunct is a food bank and a soup kitchen, called Loaves and Fishes. It gets special staffing help from the local Franciscan community.

For more information, write: Adult Day Care of Fort Worth, 1905 E. Vickery Blvd., Fort Worth, TX 76104.

Saint Benedict Health Care Center

The Benedictine Sisters opened one of the first nursing homes in Texas in 1926. In 1950 they added a hospital to the facility. After they studied programs in Great Britain and New York State (Jamaica Homes), the adult day care center was begun in 1974; its new facility was made possible through a $600,000 grant from the Economic Development Administration of the Department of Commerce. In addition, the Sisters provide an adult rehabilitative day hospital, home health care, and a hospice program.

The adult day care center of this comprehensive medical complex is housed in a separate two-story wing, located in the historic King William section of San Antonio. The first impression is one of adequate space for doing all kinds of exciting things. There are several work rooms. For example, one is assigned to ceramics with plenty of tables and its own kiln. Illumination is bright and the colors are cheerful. Music is piped in but it isn't quiet mood Muzak. The participants have made it known that they want music "their grandchildren are listening to!"

The clients are 50 percent Hispanic (a fourth of these speak only Spanish), 25 percent Black, and 25 percent Caucasian. Educational level is an average of 3.5 grades. Their average income is $314 per month; thus, the majority receive Medicaid and Medicare assistance. Private pay participants are charged $20 a day, which includes meals and craft materials. At one time, the center had ninety clients, making it one of the largest day care centers in the country, but that number is now down to a more manageable seventy-five.

The people enjoy coming. They call it "going to work," or "going to school," or "going to my club." Lynda Richardson, the resident social worker, told me most are stroke or accident victims. The majority are "Level 1s, with some Level 3s."

This bureaucratic jargon requires some explanation. Persons

requiring medical assistance through Medicaid are professionally evaluated as to the level of need. Level 1 is the minimum. Level 4 is the maximum, requiring twenty-four hour skilled care. Several years ago, when federal purse strings were tightened, individual states began reviewing nursing home populations. Those who were classified Level 1 or 2 were returned to the community, with the promise that chore care would be provided. Even a few Level 3s were denied further nursing home care. Thus, many older persons suddenly found themselves removed from a familiar, sheltered environment. This fact alone justifies the existence of adult day care centers, which provide security along with activity and medical supervision.

Richardson cites several factors that make the San Antonio facility special.

There is a dress code. People cannot come wearing pajamas or other sleepwear. People are encouraged to be well-groomed. There are electric shavers for the men, hair dryers for the women.

Incontinency is faced realistically. Each participant has an assigned locker, with a change of clothes. If there is an "accident," the person takes a shower, on the premises, and puts on the spare change of clothes. The soiled clothes are immediately washed and dried, again on the premises, and put back into the locker for the next emergency. The family is not informed. It is handled quickly and efficiently, and personal dignity is preserved.

Patients have a say in the management of their care. Rap sessions are held once a month. There are also occasional ad hoc discussions during exercise periods. Meetings with families are held twice a year. The Sisters maintain an open-door policy and do not keep secrets from clients.

Carolyn and I visited with Carmen who was making some very pretty tray favors. Some men who did not like that kind of craft work were busy with woodwork, copperware, and leather tooling. We even saw a few men doing very well at macramé.

Not all of the participants are elderly. Some are younger people who are victims of multiple sclerosis or paralysis due to accidents. We will not soon forget Roy, who answered our questions by tapping responses on a special electronic board, which we viewed through his computer's monitor screen. And there was Kim, who carefully typed her assignments on an IBM Selectric, using a stick attached to a headband. She's a college student, majoring in English, and has spent six years at Saint Benedict's.

For more information, write: Saint Benedict Health Care Center, 323 E. Johnson, San Antonio, TX 78204.

Alzheimer's Family Center, Inc.

The word *unique* is abused, but this particular adult day care center is one of a kind. I hope it will multiply across this land. It is sponsored by the Alzheimer's Disease and Related Disorders Association of San Diego.

Although Alzheimer's disease has received considerable attention in the public media in recent months, a few facts should be mentioned. It is a surprisingly common memory-loss disorder that destroys certain vital cells of the brain, which produces intellectual disability (also called *senile dementia*) in 15 percent of all individuals over age sixty-five (but it is by no means limited to persons past sixty-five). It is responsible for half of all nursing home admissions. It is estimated that 1.5 million American adults are affected, at a cost of $20 *billion* a year. Alzheimer's disease ("AD") is the fourth most common cause of death in the United States. One family out of three will see one of its parents succumb to this disease. We are one of those families. My mother, Anna, had Alzheimer's and her deterioration began at least ten years ago. The disease runs its course in from five to fifteen years.

In many cases, adult day care for Alzheimer's patients may serve as an alternative to nursing home care In some cases, it might postpone institutionalization for two or three years. Adult day care can provide relief and respite to the caregiver, if the caregiver is to maintain his or her health, happiness, and perhaps, even sanity.

The San Diego program, begun in 1982, is intended to help

AD patients and their families in four basic living situations:
1. An AD patient living with adult children.
2. An elderly couple, one of whom is the caregiving spouse.
3. An AD patient living in a foster home (called a "Board and Care" residential home in California).
4. An AD patient who comes to visit his or her family from another area. Family gatherings such as holidays often bring an AD patient into a household full of confusion, which is not what an AD patient needs. The family deserves to have some social time together, and a day care program can provide family time together without the added stress of caring for the AD member.

The first eighteen-month report of the Alzheimer's Family Center shows that 145 persons were admitted to the program. Ninety were discharged during this period, nineteen died, and eighteen were transferred to nursing homes. There were 340 individual family counseling sessions, 48 group sessions, 70 home visits involving counseling, and 50 separate sessions dealing specifically with bereavement. During this eighteen-month period, there were nearly 10,000 telephone consultations, as well as literally hundreds of various referrals to nursing homes and physicians. Special training opportunities were arranged for the medical profession. Thus, the program is truly a *family* center.

The daily program (Monday through Friday 7:30 A.M. to 5:30 P.M.) includes much personal attention, music therapy with singalongs, light exercise and gardening, cooking when permissible, parties, reality orientation, "reminiscence therapy," games, walks, rest periods, and a hot lunch and frequent snacks. Daily cost is $25.

There have been several remarkable results. One patient's confusion cleared significantly after a change of medications was recommended to the client's physician. Judy Canterbury, the registered nurse who is executive director, reports: "Much to our surprise, the vast majority of our patients improved following admission to the center. We attribute this to the lifting of the depression, coincident to the AD process, through the staff's attention and stimulus programs." Some patients began to speak again.

Others temporarily regained lost skills, such as playing the piano.

The staff ratio is one staff person to two AD participants. There are nine members on the staff. Volunteers are vital to this program. Sixty volunteers logged nearly 6,500 hours of service during a year, and others worked 2,000 hours renovating the center. They perform *all* clerical and secretarial work. They assist the professional staff with care of participants and activities. Most take CPR (Cardiopulmonary Resuscitation) certification courses. A clinical psychiatrist volunteered his time to lead twenty-four family group sessions.

The center benefits from its association with the Institute for Research on Aging. Additionally, the University of California's School of Medicine at La Jolla operates the National Alzheimer's Disease Autopsy and Brain Bank. Its purpose is threefold: *first*, an autopsy will provide a family with the only definitive diagnosis of AD; an autopsy is the only known way of verification. *Second*, if AD is not found, the remaining family members will have the knowledge that they probably will not be threatened by a genetic tendency to this disease. *Third*, unembalmed brain tissue is needed by medical researchers to further unlock the mysteries surrounding AD. (If you want more information about the Brain Bank, write University of California, Department of Pathology, M-012, School of Medicine, La Jolla, CA 92093.)

The center's annual budget is about $110,000. Its sources of income are foundations, the university, businesses, service clubs, churches, and individuals.

Without doubt, a center for Alzheimer's patients is the most difficult of adult day care centers to begin and maintain, but it fills a very great need for chronically ill AD victims and their families.

For more information, write: Alzheimer's Family Center, Inc., 3956 Third Ave., San Diego, CA 92103.

More Help for Alzheimer's Patients

Sister Patricia Murphy, president of the National Association of Activity Professionals, makes the following suggestions to persons helping AD victims. She writes primarily for activity coordinators working in nursing homes, but I believe her ideas will help anyone working in an adult day care center.

- Programming for AD residents/clients must be geared to that specific group exclusively. It is overwhelming and embarrassing for people with Alzheimer's to compete or to make sense out of general programs.
- Programs should be offered in small groups so as to identify a certain boundary of space and persons. This makes it easier for the resident/client to focus on specific groups of people in a specific place.
- Programs are successful that repeat simple actions without being condescending.
- There is a need for more assistants/volunteers (especially trained for this purpose) to assist the resident/client for each specific stage of the activity program.
- Program schedules may need to be changed to provide activities for residents/clients whose sleep patterns are reversed.
- Programs should be short in duration—twenty to thirty minutes—because of the residents'/clients' abbreviated attention span.
- Exercise programs stimulate the withdrawn patient and tone down the anxious, nervous one.
- Reminiscence is a valuable tool and should be utilized in a variety of ways. However, the same item may not spark recognition each time.
- Programs that avoid loud noises, crowds, abrupt changes, and different leaders work best for this type of resident/client.
- Action-oriented programs, where the resident/client is allowed to become involved in the process, are best. Programs that are geared toward large group entertainment allow for more mental wandering and disorientation.

Starting an Adult Day Care Center

First and foremost, join The National Institute on Adult Daycare, which was established in 1979. This is another unit of The National Council on the Aging, Inc. (600 Maryland Ave. SW, West Wing 100, Washington, DC 20024). It will put you in touch with regional groups that can help you with information and planning. It also sponsors workshops and publishes helpful books and guides.

One of these books is *Developing Adult Day Care—An Approach to Maintaining Independence for Impaired Older Persons* by Helen Padua, published by The National Council on the Aging (see address above) in 1983.

Other helpful resources are *Aging and Long-Term Care: A Directory of Selected Information Resources*, published in 1980 by the Administration on Aging, Office of Human Development Services, U.S. Department of Health and Human Services (order from the Government Printing Office, Washington, DC 20402); also, *Adult Day Care: Community Work With The Elderly* by Phillip G. Weiler and Eloise Rathbone-McCuan (New York: Springer Publishing Co., 1978).

Finally, here are some brief ideas I've culled from a variety of sources for you to consider and explore.

1. Don't start out to develop an adult day care program and end up with a senior center. Adult day care is much more difficult—and much more needed.

2. Think small, at least at the outset. You'll probably need twenty-five clients to break even; thirty to forty is a large group to manage.

3. Opt for a free-standing facility. Regulations in Texas require thirty-five square feet for each ambulatory person; fifty square feet for each nonambulatory person. Ascertain the regulations for your state from either welfare or health departments, whichever is responsible for licensing. Even if you intend to be privately supported, it will be helpful to agree to voluntary licensing and to meet the minimum standards.

There is considerable interest, chiefly from the nursing home industry, to develop adult day care centers in nursing homes. Many nursing homes have vacancies. Thus they have the room, and medical and activity personnel are available for a day care center. It seems like good use of space and specialists. However, the directors of existing adult day care centers with whom I've spoken are unanimously opposed to this idea. They say their clients are fearful of institutionalization, particularly of placement in a nursing home. Some are paranoid, even under the best of circumstances; they fear that they will be "left somewhere" or abandoned. Delivering a person to an adult center lodged in an identifiable nursing home could be traumatic and tragic.

4. Your center should be accessible for the handicapped. There should be at least one ramp at an entrance (if there are stairs), grab bars in restrooms, and sufficiently wide doors to allow for wheelchairs. If you must have carpets, choose commercial-grade installed carpeting with a short nap (avoid shag rugs!). Also select carpets of a solid color; patterns confuse and distract the frail elderly, particularly those who may have had a stroke.

5. Check with your fire marshal about required safety standards for an *educational facility*, since no overnight stay is intended. Water heaters should be checked. Smoke detectors and extinguishers are needed.

6. Install water fountains that are accessible to wheelchair participants.

7. Older people use bathroom facilities more frequently and remain there longer. You will need more restroom facilities than may be required by regulation.

8. Plan for good illumination. You will need more light than you think necessary. Avoid glare, which is especially hard on sensitive elderly eyes. Secure the help of a lighting engineer. Install clocks with extra large faces and numerals.

9. Use large type in your publicity and informational brochures. A large typewriter face such as "Orator" may be adequate. When printing, use 16 pt type.

This is an example of 16 pt type.

10. Don't invent your own training program. Learn from what others have done.

11. Consider the possibility of a Saturday and Sunday opera-

tion, either as part of a Monday-through-Friday program (making this a seven-day-per-week program) or as a weekend service only. Isolated individuals become very lonely and depressed during weekends. Caregivers need respite on weekends as well.

12. There may be problems with family members, especially from low income areas. They may not have telephones, so they cannot be easily reached in an emergency. Some will have jobs, which makes it difficult for them to take the older participant to the doctor (required once every six months by Medicaid).

Secure a written commitment from each participant and family regarding participation. How many days will the participant be attending? Which days? Will transportation be needed? What are payment arrangements? Secure consent for emergency medical care.

13. Establish a family auxiliary. This might become the nucleus of a support group for caregivers.

14. If you have any medications on the premises, keep them under lock and key.

15. Establish contact and links with existing outreach programs in your community. This will help you in making referrals, and referrals can be reciprocal.

16. Do not let mental illness or memory loss diseases overwhelm you. Padula offers good counsel: "You don't talk to or work with a diagnosis but with a person."

17. Don't expect participants to be grateful. Some will, but many, especially those who are confused and depressed, will not. We value TLC ("Tender Loving Care"), but respect may be a more realistic basis for a relationship with these older persons than TLC. Give participants a choice, whenever you can. And respect their choice.

18. Forms are a means, not an end. Don't let forms govern your life. Forms only reflect what is being *done*.

19. An adult day care center does not alter the home situation, particularly if your client lives alone. There may be repairs to be made. There probably is considerable cleaning to be done. You are not obligated to do these things yourself, but perhaps you can find agencies that can make the repairs or furnish the

chore-helpers. Part of good casework is becoming familiar with the home environment of each participant.

20. Transportation is a key component for a successful adult day care program. The next chapter deals with this need.

21. Hot noon meals should meet one-third of the daily U.S. "recommended daily allowance" of vitamins and minerals and should be low sodium and low sugar. Mid-morning and mid-afternoon snacks could be offered as well. Seek advice from a professional dietician.

22. Government funding may be available through Title XIX (Medicaid) and Title XX (both part of the Social Security Act). Contact your state department of public welfare (or human resources) for information. Federal funding may also be available through Title III of the Older Americans Act. Contact your state agency on aging for details. Additional government funding sources may become available as new legislation is enacted; your congressman can provide you with this information. Also, Councils of Governments (COGs) can help you locate information; these councils represent clusters of counties (in Austin, we relate to CAPCO—the Capital Area Planning Council—which covers a thirty-county area). (Refer to Appendix C.)

23. Private funding sources are donations, fees, business sponsorships, foundation grants, churches, service clubs, and United Way. One caution: a foundation grant is rarely given for an ongoing program. Rather, foundations mostly give "start-up" money for some specific aspect of a program. You will be fortunate if such a grant is repeated for a second or a third year. Hence, you cannot count on foundation money indefinitely; you must find alternative sources for funding, preferably during your first year of operation.

24. A medical-social adult day care model is best. This requires special licensing and employment of a full-time registered nurse or a licensed practical (or vocational) nurse. Arrangements with a physician and therapists will also be helpful; perhaps these might be secured as occasional volunteers. Therapists should be expert in physical, occupational, and speech therapies.

7

Transportation
Getting from Here to There

Transportation is important in its own right. But time and time again, providers of special services to the elderly have told me that transportation is essential to the success of their particular program. You can have an outstanding congregate meals and activity program, but unless people are able to get to what you have to offer, there isn't any benefit to them.

The focus in this book is upon the *frail* elderly, persons facing physical and emotional realities that impede their mobility. Such persons stopped driving a long time ago, if they ever drove at all. Remember that most women who are now in their seventies and eighties never learned to drive; when they were young, driving was a man's exclusive sphere and prerogative. Transportation not only meets a practical need, but also brings new excitement and zest to their lives.

Thus, *transportation* merits serious and separate consideration. It is one of the easier programs to tackle.

First, let's have a look at how older people get around.

Public Transportation

You are fortunate if your city offers some kind of public transportation. Many cities with populations of fifty thousand or less do not.

In most cases, public transportation means some kind of bus service, although larger cities may include subways, trolleys, or some form of rapid transit rail system.

74029

Consider, for a moment, the difficulties you might encounter if you were a frail or handicapped person using public transportation.

First of all, is there a route convenient to where you live? How far do you have to walk to the nearest bus or rapid transit stop?

What happens when you get to that stop? Are the schedules frequent, or will you have to wait a half-hour or more if you've missed your ride? Is service provided seven days a week? If you have to wait, is there a bench on which to sit, or shelter in case the weather suddenly brings rain or worse?

Are there stairs to climb, up or down? Are these manageable, given your handicap or lack of strength?

When the vehicle arrives, is it convenient? Can you enter at curb height, or is there a high step (or series of steps) to climb? Is a seat available near the front, if this is a bus?

Finally, does the means of public transportation take you where you need to go? Or anywhere near where you need to go?

I don't know the transportation situation where you live. But let me tell you about Austin, Texas, which is a city of a half-million. Austin provides half-fares for persons sixty-five and older, and for the handicapped; half-fares are currently only 25 cents. Also, there is a city ordinance that reserves the seats immediately behind the driver for elderly and handicapped persons. There are no lifts or ramps on its regular big buses.

However, Austin has a separate Special Transit Service. This is a fleet of five vans and five minibuses, designed for transporting elderly and handicapped people. You must register for this service and a doctor must confirm that you cannot use regular public transportation. All of these vehicles have electric or hydraulic lifts. Wheelchairs can be safely accommodated, with clamps and brackets to keep them and their passengers in place. Service is provided door-to-door, but it is not a taxi service. Usually you will share the trip with one or more persons, although there are no limitations on a destination, other than staying within the city limits. You can go to your doctor, dentist, barber, hair dresser, church, or visit a friend.

The problem is with schedule and scheduling. You must order this service in advance, by calling a special telephone number (a separate number with teletypewriter service is available for the deaf). In fact, you are well advised to request service several days before you need to keep your appointment. This is not an emergency service. And returning home may take longer than you anticipate. Often there is a long wait after you've seen your doctor or hair dresser, since others have to be picked up as well. Despite the wait, you will be driven back to your residence. Cost is minimal—only 60 cents per trip and the service is available seven days a week.

For more information about this municipal service, write Austin Transit Service, P.O. Box 1943, Austin, TX 78767.

Private Transportation for Hire

Taxis are available in most places, and, of course, they will pick you up at your door and take you directly to your destination. There is a minimum of waiting, at either end. But taxis are expensive and beyond the means of many older persons whose fixed incomes require careful budgeting.

The Yellow Cab Company in Austin has a couple of high-roof vans with lifts, which it schedules as taxis for handicapped persons, under a contract with the Texas Department of Human Resources.

Roy's Taxi Company, a local firm, has three vans for transporting handicapped persons. The minimum charge is $7 for a distance of up to five miles; fares for greater distances are negotiated.

Provider Transportation

Agencies and groups that offer special programs for older adults usually provide transportation as part of their service. They do this in several ways.

Rental Buses

Central Presbyterian Church (Austin) rents a regular-size city bus for its twice-a-month program. The bus makes stops at two retirement centers and picks up about forty passengers each time it makes its run. Highway buses (such as Greyhound or Trailways) are rented for longer out-of-town excursions. Bus rental is a line item in the church's senior adult budget.

Own Your Own

Lutheran Social Service of Texas owns two handicapped-equipped buses for its two adult day care centers in Austin. The Fort Worth adult day care center also owns its own vehicles. Churches that own vans are able to use these in older adult programs, as well as for youth and other programs.

Negotiate with Existing Transportation Programs

The Saint Benedict Health Care Center owns no vehicles of its own but has made arrangements with six different providers of transportation in San Antonio. These "providers" are either city-owned, taxi-related, or nonprofit voluntary organizations.

Many civic and church groups have chosen *transportation* to be their specific and appropriate response to serving older adults. They try to avoid duplication of services. Thus, they normally operate in a specific self-assigned area of a city.

These emerging networks of volunteer transportation providers are becoming the mainstay of other caring programs for adults. Let's look at two of them.

Care Corps

This is a volunteer ministry of the University United Methodist Church of Austin. It provides more than transportation. It visits the homebound; prepares emergency meals; helps with errands, minor household repairs, and yard work. But its major contribution is *free* transportation—helping elderly persons get to the doctor, the pharmacy, or the grocery.

The church provides a room, some office furniture, and a separate telephone line. The work is done entirely by volunteers, without any paid staff. Care Corps calls itself "a link to the church in times of need." It operates on a budget of less than $1000 a year.

Approximately sixty people commit themselves to this special ministry. Forty of them make themselves and their automobiles available on days and hours of their choice. They indicate which areas of the city they prefer to drive. A volunteer coordinator, on duty from 9 A.M. until 1 P.M., matches calls with available volunteers. An answering device takes over after 1 P.M., and several volunteer workers have beepers, which they use to check the message tape throughout the afternoon.

Training is minimal but drivers are instructed in the special needs of transporting frail and handicapped persons, especially the technique of safely transferring someone from wheelchair to car seat and vice versa. (Such training is available from visiting nurse associations, the Red Cross, and other medical professionals; the American Heart Association publishes a helpful illustrated guide.) Volunteers are members of Retired Seniors Volunteer Program which provides them with special insurance coverage in their volunteer work. (Volunteers sixty-five or over get the insurance at no cost; others pay $3 per month.)

For information about this program, write: Care Corps, University United Methodist Church, 2409 Guadalupe St., Austin, TX 78705.

Austin Volunteer Transportation Program

This transportation service is part of the United Action for the Elderly, whose Meals on Wheels program was described in Chapter 2.

Approximately 120 one-way rides a month are provided to more than two thousand frail elderly persons, using volunteer drivers and their cars. To benefit from this service, a person must be fifty-five years old or older and be unable to use public transportation (or the Special Transit Services). Service must be requested twenty-four hours in advance, and transportation is provided for medical appointments only. No charge is made but "donations from riders are appreciated," according to its promotional leaflet. The service is available Monday through Friday, from 8 A.M. until 5 P.M.

Volunteers are the key component in both Care Corps and the Austin Volunteer Transportation Program. Without volunteer drivers, many elderly persons could not get to important medical appointments. They might have to remain in a hospital or a nursing home for a longer period of time, recuperating from an illness. Volunteers also have the opportunity to visit with isolated elderly persons and assist them in other ways.

For more information about the Austin Volunteer Transportation Program, write United Action for the Elderly, P.O. Box 6235, Austin, TX 78762.

OATS—Older Adults Transportation Service

This is a showcase project from the Show-me state of Missouri.

It began in 1971, following the White House Conference on Aging, as the Cooperative Transportation Service. It required members to purchase a $1 share and pay an annual $5 membership fee. That requirement has since been discontinued. A $30,000 "seed money" grant from the Office of Aging enabled CTS to buy three buses and hire a director, a part-time secretary, and three drivers. From the outset, the program intended to serve rural as well as metropolitan areas. It began its operation in the Callaway County Courthouse in Fulton, Missouri, and offered transportation in eight surrounding counties. The name of Older Adults Transportation Service was adopted in 1973. In 1980, the name became simply OATS, Inc.

Today it serves 88 of Missouri's 114 counties as a private, nonprofit corporation. The 88 counties are divided into six geographical areas, each of which has an area office. Headquarters are in Columbia, near the center of the state. OATS owns 145 buses, employs 225 full- and part-time persons, and gets valuable support help from more than a thousand volunteers, many of whom are riders themselves. Its 1984 budget was $3 million, much of this provided under Title III-B of the Older Americans Act and a social security block grant. Additional funds come from state revenues and Urban Mass Transportation Administration allocations.

While OATS serves densely populated metropolitan areas with fixed routes, it is its rural application that is different and special, especially now that many commercial bus routes have been curtailed. One fourteen-passenger van serving an entire county is common. According to Maria Park Mueller, marketing manager of the program, a typical countywide trip would include picking up fourteen passengers, covering 150 miles during an eight-hour day, and allowing each passenger to visit the doctor, obtain medical prescriptions, have lunch, and conduct some shopping or essential business before returning home.

Riders at the beginning had to be fifty-five or older, or handicapped to the extent that they could not obtain a Missouri driver's license. The program has now been modified to provide transportation to the general public—but particularly to rural residents, the elderly, the handicapped, and low-income persons.

An annual transportation workshop is held, attended by as many as four hundred rider-volunteers, who receive professional training for their various tasks.

For further information, write: OATS, Inc., 100 E. Travis, Columbia, MO 65502.

Another Idea from Sweden

The Scandinavians, who gave us service houses, also bring us *service buses*. These special vehicles are designed strictly to meet the needs of older persons who live in rural areas. Vans are fully equipped to provide personal care, home recreational services, aids to daily living, library services, information, and distribution of food and laundry. There are usually two people who travel with the van, but sometimes there may be as many as eight. If needed, they are available to help with cleaning, housework, or minor repairs.

Steps You Could Take

1. Investigate your local public transportation program. What are its policies and services regarding the frail elderly and the handicapped? What new directions might be taken, and how can you best achieve these? Check on whether specially designed vehicles for handicapped persons are available, both from the public and the private sector. Be an advocate for comprehensive and accessible public transportation.

2. Refer to *Planning Handbook: Transportation Services for the Elderly*, published in 1975 by the former U.S. Department of Health, Education, and Welfare (Publication No. OHD76-20280). Contact the Government Printing Office (Washington, DC 20402) or your local public library for availability.

3. Learn from the experience of other volunteer transportation programs. An Adult Services Council or the ABD (Aged, Blind, and Disabled) unit of your welfare department can inform you of a nearby program.

4. Get your drivers to join the Retired Seniors Volunteer Program. The liability insurance provisions are valuable. Also, remind your volunteer drivers that they can deduct mileage or actual transportation costs when driving their own vehicles (the 1985 IRS regulations allow a 9-cents-per-mile deduction).

5. There may be other transportation programs in your city, but, as is the case with Meals on Wheels, such programs generally operate Monday-through-Friday. The elderly have transportation needs on Saturdays and Sundays as well. Perhaps this is the special way your group could help.

6. Private automobiles can provide essential transportation, but vans are often more practical because they provide more space for passengers and handicapped equipment. Providers of transportation services recommend that several smaller vehicles be secured for a transportation program, rather than one big bus. Older people tire easily and you want to try to keep travel time to a minimum. In this case, more is better and smaller is preferred.

7. Does your church have a van? If it doesn't, a van could be an excellent investment for outreach to the entire community, to

persons of all ages, within and without the church. (School bus-type vehicles may be fine for transporting children, but they aren't easily adaptable for older persons.)

Try to get a business to contribute the van. There are tax advantages to a dealer or to any commercial firm wanting to help in this special way. (Southwestern Bell contributed a van for a San Antonio program.) Nonprofit organizations may qualify for 16B2 grants (Urban Mass Transport Act) through the federal Department of Transportation. Your state highway department can provide you with additional information.

8. If your church has a van, is it equipped for the handicapped? To be handicapped equipped, your van should have some sort of ramp or lift. Also, the middle seat might be removed (or be easily removable) to allow room for a wheelchair; some sort of clamp or tie-down device is necessary to secure the wheelchair. It is helpful to have a raised roof in a van, but it isn't essential. A raised roof (or highboy) provides up to eighteen extra inches of height inside the van, which makes travel more comfortable for persons traveling in wheelchairs. Vans with raised roofs can be specially ordered, or the conversion can be done locally by automobile body shops.

Various types of ramps and lifts are available.

Mechanical lifts (hydraulic or electric) can cost $2,000 or more and must be professionally installed. Some firms to contact are:

Originator Corp., 832 NW 1st St., Ft. Lauderdale, FL 33311.

Ricon Corp., 11684 Tuxford St., Sun Valley, CA 91352.

Braun Corporation, P.O. Box 310, Winamac, IN 46996.

Names of other suppliers may be found in a current issue of *Paraplegia News*, published by the Paralyzed Veterans of America, 4350 East-West Highway, Suite 900, Bethesda, MD 20814.

Nonmechanical metal ramps range in price from $300 to $800. The least expensive are a pair of folding metal tracks, which are available in different lengths. Most will fit in a car trunk. The most expensive is a spring-weighted folding ramp which stores vertically in the side or rear door of a van. Models are available to fit the new mini-vans. Manufacturer is: Handi-Ramp Inc., P.O. Box 745, Mundelein, IL 60060. (This firm also manufactures clamps and other tie-down devices for wheel-chairs.)

9. Finally, a couple of suggestions that will add to the comfort and safety of the frail elderly who are being transported. Whenever possible, assign an extra person to accompany the driver. An aide can be very helpful in assisting the passenger from his or her home to the vehicle; this is important if the driver has other passengers and should not leave the vehicle. An aide also assists in emergencies. If the aide is a "regular," his or her familiar face and voice will reassure confused passengers.

Consider, also, the possibility of a two-way radio, linking the vehicle with the transportation office or the adult day care center. Emergency messages can be sent from the vehicle, and the driver can be informed of last-minute changes in schedule and route. This bit of modern technology facilitates travel in our crowded cities and adds a large measure of convenience and se-curity.

Transportation truly is a key component to compassionate pro-grams for the elderly. There is a gap to be filled. Groups can help. And so can individuals.

8

Protection
Legal Aid

There would appear to be no shortage of legal help for anyone living in the United States. There are some six hundred thousand lawyers and thirty-six thousand new law graduates each year. We have more lawyers per capita than any other society in the world, according to U.S. Chief Justice Warren Burger. However, the Chief Justice questions whether this surfeit of legal counsel necessarily "gives us more justice."

We have so many lawyers because we live in a bureaucracy which thrives on regulations and paper work. We also live in a litigious society. It is difficult for all older persons, but especially for the elderly poor, to cope with this legal environment. Certainly the poor and most older citizens cannot afford the $75-or-more hourly consultation fees, not to mention the costs of preparing and presenting a case in court.

Older people sometimes need help with securing benefits, whether social security or private pension plans, or a combination of both. Medicare decisions may need to be challenged. Protective services run the gamut from establishing some kind of limited power-of-attorney, to actual guardianship, to possible commitment to a mental institution. The individual's rights must also be protected where there is fraud or other consumer abuse. Older persons divorce each other or sometimes abandon each other.Wills of older persons often need review, as spouses and other beneficiaries die and other life situations change. Legal counsel is vital.

Free legal services help, where they are available.

Legal Aid Societies began in 1876. The first one was established in New York City to improve the living situation of German immigrants. A small network emerged in other cities where immigrants settled. Today, more than a century later, Legal Aid Societies provide a broad spectrum of legal services to persons from all segments of society.

The Office of Economic Opportunity, established in 1964, initiated some three hundred legal service programs. During President Richard Nixon's administration, this program evolved into the *Legal Services Corporation*, established as "an independent nonprofit corporation, funded by the Congress, with a board appointed by the President." The program expanded into all fifty states during Carter's administration. Again using Texas as an example, there are eleven legal service programs, as well as a statewide support and training program.

Some of the local programs are related to established legal aid societies. Others are innovative programs, such as legal clinics or neighborhood "first aid" legal offices. The budget of the Legal Services Corporation was cut 25 percent during President Reagan's first administration; but the loss has been made up in some places by funds from city, county, United Way, law schools, and other sources. The Congress did not confirm any of Reagan's appointees to the corporation board during his first administration. The issue has become highly politicized and controversial.

Questions of strategy and tactics remain. Should legal services be provided to everyone as a right? If they are, how should the services be delivered? And how, then, should the actual legal services be handled? Such questions raise policy considerations and have political overtones.

Despite the cutbacks in federal funding, legal help is available, if older people know where to look. The Legal Aid Society of Central Texas, for example, functions in two areas.

First, it provides free service through the Senior Citizens' Law Project to anyone who is sixty or older regarding certain rights and benefits. It assists in questions of Medicare and Medicaid, guardianship where it is necessary for the protection of older persons, nursing home complaints, elderly housing issues, food stamps, social security and SSI (Supplemental Security Income), and veterans' benefits.

Second, older persons who meet certain low-income guidelines qualify for free legal service in matters involving wills, probate, small claims and consumer problems, divorce, suspension of a driver's license, and power of attorney. If a person is past sixty, living on a fixed income that is modest but above federal guidelines, that person has to pay for such legal services or do without.

In Dallas County (Texas), older Americans living in rural areas don't have to go to a legal aid office; the legal office comes to them. More than fifteen hundred seniors benefit each year from the *Older Americans Legal Action Center* van, which is equipped with filing cabinets, desks, typewriter, and office supplies. Three full-time and two part-time attorneys assist isolated older persons in general civil cases, with wills, and legal protective services where there may have been exploitation, physical abuse, or self-neglect. Often the roving staff refers routine legal work to retired lawyers who volunteer for this purpose.

There is still another recourse. Many lawyers recognize the unfairness of the guidelines and provide free legal assistance to persons just above the poverty line. They do this through an American Bar Association project called *Pro Bono Publico*, which means "for the good of the public." To finance such programs, many lawyers are contributing the interest earned on escrow or other restricted accounts over which they have temporary jurisdiction.

Bruce J. Terris, former assistant to the Solicitor General and an attorney who has represented the elderly in issues affecting housing care, urges action, especially from community groups.

There can be little doubt that the elderly poor urgently need and can significantly benefit from a substantially greater degree of legal assistance than is now available. Legal assistance for them is even more scarce than for the younger poor. While lawyers can not perform miracles, they can protect the elderly from injustices and can develop new kinds of affirmative programs to benefit them. The elderly, *and most especially those who work with the elderly* (italics mine), have a responsibility to develop new legal service programs and obtain the resources to implement them. Only in this way can the aged be guaranteed justice. (From *Legal Services for the Elderly*, published by The National Council on the Aging, Inc.)

As you survey your community and meet with older persons, you are bound to hear about certain situations that require legal assistance. If you decide to develop some kind of community program, *referral* to other agencies, including legal aid agencies, will be an important part of that program.

What can you do?

1. You must be sure of the need. A census, or survey, of your community cannot be overemphasized.

2. Determine what *free* legal help is presently available. Is legal help provided in your region through the Legal Services Corporation? Check with your city, county, or area Legal Aid Society. Ask about referral services at your state or local Bar Association. Call your local Civil Liberties Union office for other suggestions.

3. Secure or borrow the following publication: *Legal Services for the Elderly* by Bruce J. Terris, published by The National Council on the Aging, Inc., 600 Maryland Ave., SW, West Wing 100, Washington, DC 20024. This monograph was last reprinted in 1975. Although some of the information is now out-of-date, its ideas and suggestions are still quite relevant.

4. Contact the Pro Bono Publico Project of the American Bar Association, 1705 DeSales St., NW, Washington, DC 20036. Ask about *public good* services in your area.

5. If no free legal aid program exists in your community, bring together a few lawyers to discuss the need and possibilities for meeting it. Advocacy is the role of an *advocate*, which is a synonym for *lawyer* or *counselor*. Perhaps some kind of legal clinic could be established. Recent law school graduates may welcome the opportunity to meet directly with a variety of clients and to deal with a variety of issues. However, the guidance and participation of older experienced and established attorneys is also needed.

6. Once you determine what free legal aid is available (or may

become available), alert the elderly persons in your community about this availability. There aren't many roving legal vans, as in Dallas County, and lawyers don't normally make any more "house calls" than doctors. Clients have to make their way to their local Legal Aid Society or Legal Clinic, since telephone contacts are discouraged and sometimes refused. Thus, an *outreach program* that informs people about available legal aid must precede the legal aid itself.

Postscript

We've been discussing free legal aid for *individuals*. But attorneys can also help older individuals by helping groups and organizations that seek to aid the elderly. Some of these services could be contributed; fees will doubtless have to be charged for others. But concerned legal professionals can help in significant ways, and they are needed.

Examples:

Incorporation. Community agencies need to establish nonprofit corporation status. They need legal help and usually cannot afford to pay for it.

Lawyers can also help local senior citizen groups to become nonprofit corporations. Many of these groups manufacture items for sale or establish retail outlets in housing projects.

Housing. Legal help is essential in developing housing projects for the elderly, whether with federal or private funding.

Legislation. Attorneys obtained passage of a rent-control ordinance in Miami Beach, which protected a large number of elderly tenants from rent increases. In Massachusetts, lawyers helped secure legislation that assured common kitchen and dining areas to be built in all state-aided public housing.

Representation. Senior citizen groups often require public advocates (call them lobbyists, if you prefer) to interpret needs and promote solutions. Persons who understand both the legal and the political system can help.

Board Membership. Voluntary agencies need all of the expertise they can get. Persons with legal background and experience can help such agencies avoid problems, as well as solve them.

9
Routine and Order
Helping Hands — Practical Serving Projects

At the outset of this book we discussed the importance of identifying the needs of older persons, as illustrated in Dr. Abraham H. Maslow's "inverted pyramid." One of those basic needs, second in importance to physiological or body needs, is *security*. Security encompasses protection from threat, danger, and illness. It includes shelter, routine, order, rhythm, and predictability. In the preceding chapters of Part Two, we have seen many examples of compassionate response to these basic needs.

This chapter summarizes "all of the above" by looking at several comprehensive and multiservice programs. Despite their emphasis on statistics, census tracts, and organization, these kinds of programs ultimately show how one person cares for another, and how that action can make a significant difference in an elderly person's quality of life. This reminds me of the answer Jim MacCracken, former director of Church World Service, gave to the question: "How can anyone really do anything about world hunger?" Jim replied, "You do it by helping one person at a time."

Each of us can offer our helping hands.

A major catalyst in the community help movement for the elderly is the Robert Wood Johnson Foundation of Princeton, New Jersey, the nation's largest health foundation, which, since 1972, has distributed more than $550 million to improve health care in the United States. (The Interfaith Volunteer Caregivers Program of the Robert Wood Johnson Foundation is administered by the Benedictine Hospital, P.O. Box 1939, Kingston, NY 12401.)

In 1983, the foundation announced a new *Interfaith Caregivers Program*, in cooperation with the National Interfaith Coalition on Aging. It invited applications from interfaith coalitions of churches and synagogues for three-year pilot programs that would recruit and train volunteers to "provide assistance to the health-impaired in ways that will enable them to remain in their community." Nearly one thousand coalitions responded to the initial call; of these, 345 submitted proposals. In March 1984 grants totalling $3.8 million were announced to 25 of these groups, located in seventeen states, the District of Columbia, and Guam. Their names and locations are listed in Appendix D.

The motivation behind the grants is that religious organizations have a unique capacity to enhance support programs and arrangements. "With 120 million Americans as active churchgoers, many of whom are elderly, churches and synagogues have the opportunity to identify and care for vulnerable individuals in their communities through already-established communications networks among their members." (Quotation from the Foundation's initial prospectus.)

The scope of this project is astounding. Among the twenty-five "winners" are more than six hundred congregations, working together, representing not only Christian and Jewish communities, but also Islam, Bahai, Buddhists, and an indigenous Native American religious group. It is estimated that nearly ten thousand frail and "at risk" older persons will be served and helped in these twenty-five neighborhood programs by more than six thousand trained volunteers.

The menu of services to be offered is equally exciting and, in a way, is a summary of many of the service opportunities described in this book.

Some of the projects give special emphasis to *needs assessment*—a comprehensive, organized statement of older persons' needs for specific services.

Service management is defined as matching needs for services with priority given to the greatest, most critical needs—linking disabled persons to available services in the community.

Under *Basic Living Services*, the following categories are listed:

Homecare/Homemaking
Meal Preparation/Delivery
Friendly Visiting/Companionship
Telephone Reassurance
Transportation
Shopping
Chore Care

Personal Care Services are described as:

Dressing
Bathing
Hair Shampooing
Feeding
Toileting
Ambulating (helping persons to walk; exercising)
Giving Respite to Caregivers

Special attention in all twenty-five programs will be given to *caregivers support groups*—providing ideas and support for preventing problems, maintaining health ("wellness"), and suggesting ways to avoid strain for both the caregiver and the care receiver.

The program also includes *hospice* care, which provides physical, emotional, and spiritual help to terminally ill persons and their families.

Each of the twenty-five groups will receive $50,000 a year for three years, to demonstrate whether this kind of comprehensive volunteer-based program is viable and achievable.

A program in San Antonio suggests that it will work.

CO-OP

CO-OP (Community Outreach for Older Persons) was one of the twenty-five 1984 Robert Wood Johnson Foundation grantees, but its work began in 1980 and already has a track record. Its director is Mollie Fleming, who is a social worker.

Originally housed in Morningside Manor, a retirement center

sponsored by three denominations, CO-OP now has its office in one of the twelve sponsoring churches. Its outreach is limited to the Jefferson area of San Antonio, where census tracts indicated a substantial elderly population.

The project grew out of a concern of the San Antonio Urban Council, a church-related social action consortium. A survey of the neighborhood was attempted, with mixed success. Volunteers learned that the Jefferson area had a high incidence of burglaries, and residents (especially older ones) were fearful and reluctant to answer questions. The twelve participating churches then carefully surveyed their own older adult members, and the results were pooled and correlated.

As the program developed, information about it was disseminated through posters in supermarkets and laundromats, on car cards in buses, through public service announcements on radio and TV, and in local congregations.

From the beginning, it was assumed that both clients and volunteer workers would have to be recruited simultaneously.

Eight programs are now in place, based on the results of the church-neighborhood survey and follow-up discussion and planning. Note the priorities that the San Antonio group chose.

1. *Nutrition*. Meals are delivered to persons who are recuperating in their homes from illness, accident, or operation. Social workers in the hospitals alert CO-OP to patients being discharged who need such help. Also, "Senior Lunch/Brunch" programs were begun in each of the twelve sponsoring churches.

2. *Health care*. This is not yet a full home health care program but volunteer visitors are involved with *preventive* care. Blood pressure is taken and monitored. Health literature, of special importance to older persons, is distributed.

3. A *widowhood support group*. A psychologist and his wife volunteered to work with this group.

4. A *caregivers support group*. From the outset, its purpose was to be self-training through sharing, with occasional outside leadership. What can caregivers actually *do* in specific situations? How can they help each other?

5. *Social contacts*. Telephone reassurance volunteers were en-

listed and trained. Classes were begun for persons who were not homebound; the subjects were selected on the basis of the finding of its survey.

6. *Repair services*. The people of the CO-OP learned that spring was the busiest time for minor repairs in homes and apartments of elderly people. They also learned that even changing a light bulb was important, because by just being inside a home or apartment, the helper had a chance to note other things that needed repair, or that needed correcting for reasons of safety. A common discovery was that rugs needed to be tacked down at doorways.

7. *Referrals*. Once a month, representatives from all social service agencies in San Antonio get together for an informal meeting. This sharing of program ideas and progress is helpful to each agency, establishes linkages, and provides current information for referrals. CO-OP volunteers routinely refer elderly persons to other health, social service, insurance, and legal contacts.

8. *Counseling*. As one-to-one relationships develop, volunteers not only refer clients elsewhere but become available listeners. They offer counsel as each is able, or they suggest professional counseling when this need is evident.

Supporting each of the preceding eight programs is *transportation*.

Approximately two hundred people are being helped through these programs. Services to clients are free but, as in similar programs, they are encouraged to contribute when they can.

Since the program began, eighty volunteers have been recruited, fifty of whom are regular participants. Their training began with a briefing session about the program, at which time special interests and skills of volunteers were identified, and for which future training sessions were planned.

The first need was to staff the office, which was an empty room with a telephone. Training was given in routine office management and how to handle the expected influx of a variety of telephone inquiries. Volunteers brought their own typewriters to these sessions!

Quarterly and now monthly meetings with volunteers are held to share ideas and experiences over a cup of coffee or tea. Visiting experts and leaders help volunteers better understand the basic facts of aging, nutrition, and such practical matters as how to transfer a person from a wheelchair to a car.

Future goals include more recruitment of volunteers and churches. There are forty-three churches in the Jefferson area, but only twelve, thus far, are officially part of CO-OP. There is also a need to find additional funding, since the foundation grant expires in 1987. The CO-OP board, representing the participating churches, believes that the program should continue for an additional three years, through 1990. It is raising reserve funds now, toward the day when the programs must become self-supporting.

Mollie Fleming cautions that when you begin this kind of program you have to decide that you can't do everything. You have to be selective and practical. When you offer transportation, for example, do you offer it unconditionally, regardless of destination? Do you limit it only to medical need (as do most transportation programs)? Or will you allow an occasional visit to a beauty shop, which could greatly raise morale and self-image? You must establish your guidelines ahead of time. Fleming and her board have definitely ruled out "sitting" assignments, convinced that volunteers' time is limited and must be shared (needs for companions are referred to other agencies). "You can kill a program," says Mollie, "if you 'overload' it."

For more information, write: CO-OP, c/o Grace Presbyterian Church, 950 Donaldson, San Antonio, TX 78228.

There is an interesting postscript to this program. An ecumenical group in Austin submitted a proposal to the Robert Wood Johnson Foundation and didn't make the cut. The need didn't go away, and neither did the idea. Six churches have agreed to organize the *West Austin Caregivers*. One church will provide office space and a telephone. A volunteer director has been secured, who will use her experience as her practicum toward a Master of Social Work degree. The group begins its multiservice program with an annual budget of only $1,500. Mollie Fleming has visited the Austin group, and several Austinites have gone to San Antonio to observe the CO-OP venture. Thus an idea and a venture grow.

Home Again Program

Caregiving programs sometimes divide, sometimes multiply. The *Home Again* program is a spin-off from the Meals on Wheels project in Cheyenne, Wyoming. It discovered a special need for older recuperating adults who were leaving a hospital and returning to their homes, and who had no available or visible help from family or friends. Obviously, a special support system was needed. Home Again began in the fall of 1984.

The format is simple. A volunteer visits the patient in the hospital before his or her discharge. On the day of discharge, the volunteer transports the patient home. For at least the next two weeks, there is daily follow-up by the volunteer, providing friendly services and running errands to assure the patient's comfort and safety. And, of course, hot nutritious meals are delivered through Meals on Wheels.

Most of the actual work takes place on the day of hospital discharge. The kitchen and bathroom are cleaned. Fresh groceries are purchased and put away. Bed linen is checked and changed, if necessary. The volunteer offers to take soiled linen home to launder. If needed, the volunteer picks up prescriptions and any required health appliances.

Dee Clary, executive director of Cheyenne's Meals on Wheels, articulated the need for this kind of program in her letter to local pastors:

> As people live longer, our elderly population is growing at a phenomenal rate. As a result of Medicare cutbacks, many needy men and women return home from hospitals and other health care facilities after shorter stays. We are asking that you consider carefully a church "Home Again" project, in cooperation with Meals on Wheels. Our agency will provide the volunteer training and coordinate referrals made to us by Discharge Personnel at the health agencies....We recognize that churches give extra support and encouragement to their members during illness; ours is a planned extension of this [support],

offering practical assistance to those returning home to recuperate. The program is endorsed by Cheyenne's Coalition of Agencies Serving the Elderly (CASE) as a needed service not duplicated by any other agency.

Doctors were also alerted to the positive benefits to patients from this program.

The training program includes an explanation and rationale of Home Again, some basic understanding of the elderly (with special attention to an older person's response to losses of all kinds), a walk-through of the Home Again process, both before discharge and on the day of discharge, a discussion of the rights and responsibilities of the volunteers (including liability and safeguards). Confidentiality of the patient's situation is stressed.

The program receives no federal money and is community-funded. The United Way provides 20 percent of the budget. The city and county each provide 5 percent. The remainder comes from contributions from businesses, churches, service clubs, and individuals.

For information about this innovative new program, write: Meals on Wheels of Cheyenne, Inc., P.O. Box 1496, Cheyenne, WY 82003-1496.

Community Care Program

This program, based in Honolulu, goes beyond Home Again. It, too, is concerned about persons who need special assistance during recuperation, but it is designed for elderly persons who do not have a home to which they can return, or who would be unable to manage for themselves in their own home. The key to this program is the *foster home* and the *foster family*.

This program was begun in 1979 by Queen's Medical Center, through its Department of Social Work. Hospital authorities were troubled about the growing number of patients waiting in the acute care hospital for a vacant nursing home bed. Hospital personnel recognized that many of the elderly persons in need of intermediate care did not need to be institutionalized, if there were trained caregivers (families) to meet the patients' needs. Hospital staff investigated similar home placement programs developed by Massachusetts General Hospital in Boston and Johns Hopkins Hospital in Baltimore.

Since this program began, more than sixty patients have been placed with foster families, who are carefully screened and are trained for their special role. The program is intergenerational, but in Hawaii, it is also multiracial. Foster families receive monthly stipends ranging from $400 to $700, depending upon the client's level of disability. That money comes from the client's social security benefits, supplemented by local foundation grants.

For information, write: Community Care Program, Queen's Medical Center, P.O. Box 861, Honolulu, HI 96908.

The Errand Service, Inc.

Meanwhile, "back on the ranch in Texas," a former adult day care center director has started a nonprofit venture called *The Errand Service.*

Donna Loflin describes it as an agency that provides various support services to the homebound elderly. One telephone call from a client and Donna and her crew of volunteers will do the shopping, go to the bank, pay a bill, assist with forms and insurance, secure special transportation, provide information, and make referrals. The Errand Service does the things the homebound older person is unable to do.

The clients must be elderly and at least partially disabled. They must apply for the service, but that's a simple process and can be done by telephone. All income levels are welcomed. Fees are based on a sliding scale, depending on the individual's ability to pay. All clients are expected to contribute something to help cover the cost of the services. Private supporters make up the difference.

For information, write: The Errand Service, Inc., 2813 Glenview, Austin, TX 78703.

Donna's goal is "to enhance the independence and well-being of the homebound elderly by providing hard-to-find support services at affordable rates. Many of our clients," she says, "would have to give up their independence and move into nursing homes, were it not for the availability of these services."

That's obviously the purpose of all of the alternative, helping-hands, compassionate ministries described in this chapter.

Part Three

Meeting Basic Emotional Needs

10

Belonging
Pastoral Ministries

Not too long ago a retired high school teacher stood up in the church I attend and said, "You have all these programs for the kids; when are you going to do something about us? You have a person working almost full-time with youth; *what about us*?!" My friend, Franklyn Zinn, was smiling, but he was dead serious about his concern.

That's what this chapter is about: how four churches discovered new ways to minister to senior adults. Check those areas and programs that apply to your situation. At the close of this chapter are suggestions on how to build on those notes and begin a pastoral ministry with older adults in your congregation.

First Presbyterian Church
Bryan, Texas

The city of Bryan (population 45,000) is next door to College Station (population 40,000), the home of Texas A&M University. It is a stable, prosperous community, with a small-town environment and the lowest unemployment rate in the state. Many of its citizens are retired university professors. Thus, the Bryan/College Station community, in addition to being prosperous, is literate and prone to probe and venture.

Several years ago, Bryan's First Presbyterian Church received a rather large bequest that was specifically earmarked for "service to the community." The money was not to be used to enlarge the institution nor to buy new equipment. In traditional Presbyterian fashion, the Session referred this challenge to a committee, in this case its Witness Committee. That committee felt that something needed to be done about and for its older members, so it, in turn, decided to appoint a Task Force on Aging. At this early stage it was only a *feeling*. Facts were needed.

The Task Force consisted of eight members, representing the age spectrum from youth to retirees. It gave itself three months to do its job. And it accepted these objectives for its study:

- To make the congregation more aware of the needs and problems of its older members;
- To identify the older members of the church;
- To determine what community and church resources are presently available to these members;
- Through the means of a survey to identify the needs of older members and analyze those needs;
- To make recommendations on ways the church might satisfy any existing needs.

The group learned that in this congregation of 700 members, 162 were retired or over the age of sixty-five. This was nearly one-fourth of the membership. The Task Force then determined to interview each of these 162 persons. That didn't quite work out, even though additional interviewers were recruited and trained. Some people were traveling; others were ill. However, eighty-one interviews were completed.

An interesting profile emerged of this particular congregation's older population. Fifty-five percent were married; 37 percent were single or widowed; 67 percent had completed college, a very high rate considering that most of the respondents would have entered college during the depression. Eighty percent owned their own homes and cars. Eighty-eight percent felt they had an adequate income for the present and future. Eighty-eight percent said they had dependable help nearby; 68 percent had daily telephone contact with someone. Ninety-six percent had hobbies; 75 percent had "interests" at home. Seventy-five percent declared they were in good health; the rest, 25 percent, said they had health problems such as hearing and visual difficulties. Only 47 percent attended weekly worship services. Forty-five percent belonged to retirement organizations; the rest, apparently, couldn't have cared less.

What kinds of concerns might such a self-sufficient group have?

The survey revealed that 25 percent of these persons had difficulty performing their own repairs around the home. Fourteen percent felt their talents and interests were not being used by the church. Again, 14 percent felt the church had not responded to them in times of need. Ten percent felt the church did not provide help regarding the processes of aging and dying. And there was this important finding: 37 percent of the persons surveyed seldom visited family and friends away from home.

The Task Force completed its work within three months and made seven recommendations to the Session, the governing body of the congregation.

First, it recommended that transportation be provided to older members, either by the church and/or community programs, particularly for programs held at night, when many elderly persons prefer not to drive. The church already owned a van, and its use could be expanded.

Then other recommendations dealt with more communication from the church to older members about church programs, that an inventory be made of talents and skills of older members, that a special ministry be developed for shut-ins and nursing home residents, that a volunteer network be established to help with repairs or errands, that special classes and events be designed for older members, and that church facilities be made barrier-free. Key to several of these recommendations was the conviction that a part-time director would have to be employed to coordinate this program.

One of the members of the Task Force was employed as that part-time director. Pat Baker brought nearly a decade of experience as a worker in senior adult programs. She was also a member of the church and already knew many of its older members.

Pat was an excellent choice, even though she is a relatively young person and has had to build rapport and trust with the older members. She has been at her job for more than two years, and she is now accepted. Officially, she works twenty hours a week. Unofficially, she's on call every day—and she enjoys it.

Her first action was to establish an advisory council, made up of older adults. Pat's philosophy of programming is clearly seen in her title: "Coordinator of Services with Older Adults." Note that it is *with* adults, not *for* or *to* adults. The advisory council reports to the Service Committee, which, in turn, is accountable to the Session (or *church council*, as it might be called in other congregations).

Despite her considerable experience in working with older adults, Pat says she has had to learn by trial and error. "Some of the things the council suggested which I thought wouldn't work, did," she says. "Some of things I was completely convinced would work, didn't."

Pat Baker and the advisory council opted for quality, not quantity. They also agreed on some things they didn't want. They didn't want a regular luncheon program; the city of Bryan has a superfluity of luncheon programs for poor and wealthy alike. They also decided against craft and games programs; again, the community offered these and there was no need to duplicate activities and effort. There was value, they believed, in maintaining relationships with ongoing programs in the community.

In fact, Baker saw her main job to be "a link between the older people in the church and the community." Hence, part of her task is to be a resource person—to let people know what is happening in the community politically, socially, and medically.

Even though the council did not want a luncheon program, there are now some shared meals, but these are only held once a quarter. They discovered a need for older members to socialize once in a while. At first this meant a meal, followed by bingo. Now it is a luncheon tied in with continuing education.

One of the first such luncheons was a salt-free meal, with each member bringing a covered dish. Baker now recalls that the result was pretty horrible, and everyone went out for pizza afterwards. However, a nutritionist was a guest and spoke about the need for reducing salt in diets, especially for older persons, and suggested some ways to make salt-free food more palatable. The next luncheon, held during Christmas season, was sugar-free.

A summer luncheon featured only salads and fruit. A local band, dubbed "The Medicare Jazz Band," played themselves ragged. After the musicians left, everyone continued to entertain themselves around the piano and organ.

The recommendation about communication is being carried out in several ways. The weekly church newsletter includes a column called "Vantage Point," which provides information to older adults. There is a monthly newsletter just for the older members. And the pastor, Dr. Robert Leslie, prepares a weekly radio broadcast targeted for the homebound and roombound.

The church library was expanded to include large-print devotional books. One church visitor, herself eighty-five years old (and about whom we'll learn more in a moment), circulated these and other books as she made her rounds.

This reservoir of experience is tapped for leadership and help both in the church and the community. A couple of slogans emphasize the idea: "Our Elders Have Done It Longer" and "Recycle Experience: Hire an Elder."

A special section in the church library was developed especially for caregivers. It includes materials on aging, travel ideas (especially to nearby places in Texas), and an ample file on local resources (items on nutrition and home health care agencies, for example).

Seminars for older adults were planned. These were not brief one-hour programs, but in-depth classes that required a commitment of two hours a day twice a week, for two weeks. The seminars have the umbrella name of "The World Beyond Bryan/College Station," which allows plenty of latitude for topics.

The first seminar was on travel, conducted by local travel agents. It provided practical help for planning a trip to anywhere in the world. Many of these older adults had traveled frequently during their working years but now needed to update their knowledge.

A second seminar was on computers. A retired professor

brought his home minicomputer system and gave hands-on instruction about the benefits computers have for older people in their homes. Not many computer systems were sold, but one person said, "I just don't want to grow old not knowing about computers." Another participant said, "My grandchildren know all about computers; I need to know something about them, too, so we can talk together about them."

A future seminar will be on the arts—not just painting or ceramics, but exploring different kinds of creative arts. One instructor will be a local poet who is one of the older members.

Pat Baker admits that these seminars haven't attracted huge groups of people, but although the groups are small, they are active and *interested* groups.

She is doing something similar for caregivers. She calls these courses "Help for Families of the Aging." They are held every quarter and require a commitment by participants to attend sessions two evenings a week for eleven weeks.

The first group had only five members. The second grew to thirteen. The sessions begin at 7:30 P.M., but those who are interested may come a half-hour earlier to explore some of the special problems in caring for persons who have Alzheimer's or other memory-loss diseases, or those who have hearing or eyesight loss. The study groups have also become support groups.

Two interesting spin-off clusters have evolved from this more informed understanding of caring for each other. One is a *Lifestyle* support group for widows and widowers. From that group emerged one called *Compassionate Friends*, a support group for parents whose children have died.

Pat says more older people are "coming out of the closet," admitting that they do need help in special ways. Often these pleas for help come on her days off, usually by telephone to her home. Thus there is now more person-to-person counseling than when this special ministry began.

Horizons are widened not only by study and conversation, but also through travel. Many of these older Presbyterians had visited Europe, but had never been to a tiny rural Lutheran church in Brenham, just forty miles away. That church has been blessed with an unusually beautiful pipe organ. So a day trip was arranged, taking the church van and fourteen passengers. The pastor, who is an accomplished musician, went along to provide the concert.

Overnight trips have become popular. The group has gone to Houston and Fort Worth to view traveling exhibits from China or Native American art. An excursion to Granbury and its opera, located near Fort Worth, is always popular. Another trip has taken them to the famous YO Ranch in Mountain Home, in the Texas hill country, to see the largest existing herd of longhorn cattle.

Wherever possible, they stay in older homes or vintage hotels. These trips require lots of planning because so many logistical details are involved. However, the trips are initially chosen by the older adults themselves; they make it clear where they want to go. This year there will be six daytime trips and four overnighters, which isn't too bad for a part-time program!

Other churches are beginning to hear about the program and are asking for consultation and advice. Since there are eighty-two churches in the Bryan/College Station vicinity, each with a significant number of older adults, much can be done together.

But this isn't the end of the story.

Pat has done some very special things to introduce her older friends to the congregation. *Introduce* may appear to be a strange word when many of these people have been members of this particular congregation for six decades or more. Nevertheless, Pat found a way to make a connection between the generations.

One project was a "Beautiful Baby Contest." Older members were asked to bring in a baby picture of themselves. "You're never too old to win a beauty contest!" they were told. The group loved the idea. One gentleman, a member of the church for thirty-four years, who hadn't been particularly involved with the older adult activities, was the first to submit a baby photograph.

The pictures were displayed and identified by number, not by name. The members of the congregation were asked to vote for their favorite and the results were announced the following Sunday. The first place winner and two runners-up were given prize trophies: a bare baby lying on tummy, with inscription.

Since 1983 was designated by the Presbyterian denomination as "the year of the older person," Baker asked her council to nominate a dozen older persons who had made a significant contribution to the church and to the community, both in the past and the present. One person would be featured each month. The council chose thirteen—nine singles and four couples—and called it a "Baker's Dozen," with pun intended.

Announcement was made in the weekly church newsletter. Each nominee was asked to provide photographs and other small items which would describe his or her life. These were placed in a special glass display case, with captions, as a kind of "this is your life" diorama. Pat reports that each month's display got better as the new honoree saw what the previous person had done. The display just outside the sanctuary was a popular spot for the entire congregation. The photos, ranging from infancy to adulthood, naturally included weddings and other important events. One young person was heard to exclaim, "Wow, I didn't know she looked like that at my age!" Another murmured, "And all this time I thought I was just talking to a hearing aid!"

Recognition was given to the monthly recipient during a morning worship service, giving thanks to God for the life and work of this particular "servant." A bulletin insert provided more information about the individual. A certificate of remembrance was presented.

The congregation got to know seventeen of its older members in this intimate and refreshing way. Let me share the information about Frances Lowry Barber, which appeared in the bulletin insert on the day she was honored. She's that eighty-five-years-young church visitor mentioned earlier.

FRANCES LOWRY BARBER

Frances Barber, a native Texan of 84 years, was born at the jailhouse in Jacksboro, Texas. To qualify her birthplace, it just happened that the only available housing for a city employee at that time was the apartment above the jail.

She grew up in Waxahachie, Dallas, and Jacksonville, Texas,

where she met her husband, George Lincoln Barber, and spent most of her 40 married years. They have five children, two sons and three daughters. Their children have blessed them with fifteen grandchildren and numerous great-grandchildren. All of her children now live in Texas.

Frances grew up in the Methodist Church and did not become a Presbyterian until she joined this church in October 1963. Her early memories of church work include teaching Sunday School at the age of fourteen and, later, her daughter's high school class, where she thinks she learned as much as they did. She was the first woman to be ordained an elder in First Presbyterian Church.

Frances became the church caller for this church in 1964. Her main job at that time was visiting prospective members in the community. As the years passed, this volunteer job has taken on many facets. On Monday mornings the sign-in sheets from the fellowship folders are on her desk, and the struggle begins trying to decipher everyone's handwriting. From these sheets she makes a list of visitors to be passed on to the pastor and the other church callers. She then records the members' attendance in the roll books. Besides the hours of paperwork, the most important service to her is the visitation she does each week to shut-ins, hospital patients, and people in nursing homes. Frances also keeps the bulletin board with newspaper clippings of the activities of our members.

Her past service to the community includes many service organizations and an active membership in the Bryan Garden Club.

Frances is honored today as an Older Person who unselfishly gives hour after hour to others in the church and community in need of a hand to hold or just a kind word.

Now you know Frances Lowry Barber as well!

The citation she and the other honorees received bears this inscription:

The Session, the Clergy, and Older Adults
of
First Presbyterian Church
recognize

_____

for life-long devotion to Christian giving of
self, love, and life, serving as a living example
of the love of OUR LORD.

Obviously, Baker puts in many more hours than the twenty hours per week for which she is paid. She loves the work and the people with whom she works. Although she brought lots of professional knowledge and experience to her job, she wishes she had known more about a congregation-based ministry to older adults. She has learned from on-the-job training. And for beginning such a ministry the congregation as a whole is much happier today, she affirms.

Her denomination now has an Office on Aging, and *enablers* for this ministry are being placed in each presbytery. Workshops are held. Materials are prepared, including a national monthly newsletter which is an information exchange. The Presbyterian School of Christian Education in Richmond, Virginia, offers an intensive two-day course through its Center on Aging for persons exploring the challenge of ministry to older persons in a local congregation.

Pat's program operates on an annual budget of less than $10,000. With the involvement of trained volunteers as administrators, she feels a similar program could be carried out with a yearly expenditure of only $2,000.

For more information about this program write: First Presbyterian Church, 1100 Carter Creek Parkway, Bryan, TX 77801.

Park Cities Baptist Church
Dallas, Texas

Dallas—"Big D"—is very different from Bryan/College Station; and Park Cities Baptist Church is one of those huge, almost overwhelming, square-city-block, tall-steeple Southern Baptist complexes. It is located in north central Dallas, surrounded by a mammoth shopping mall, high-rise condominiums, and well-maintained older residences.

Park Cities Baptist Church has seven thousand members. Fifteen hundred of these are older adults, persons who are sixty years old or older. It is a multistaff, multiservice congregation. Its members live throughout the city.

Its Minister to Senior Adults is a layperson, Gena Hestand. She is married to a retired army officer. Several years ago she felt the call to full-time professional Christian service and completed graduate work at the Central Baptist Theological Seminary in Kansas City. She brings a wealth of experience and commitment to her present work.

Park Cities, as we said, is a multiservice congregation. In the fine-tuned, well-organized tradition of Southern Baptists, this congregation had comprehensive programs for young and middle adults, single adults, youth, children, and preschoolers—but nothing for senior adults.

One of those seniors attended a workshop on starting such a ministry at Baylor University, and returned to Park Cities with enthusiasm and energy to begin something in his Dallas church. After all, there were fifteen hundred older members in the church, which anywhere else would be a congregation in its own right.

A Senior Adult Council was formed with fifteen members, representing different existing organizations in the church (men's Bible class, women's mission groups, etc.). Five members rotate off the council every six months, so there is constant fresh input to the group, which then determines the program it wants.

Together with Hestand, who had now been employed by the congregation to work with senior adults, the council studied Horace L. Kerr's book *How to Minister to Senior Adults in Your Church* (Broadman Press, 1980). Dr. Kerr gives good advice about interviewing techniques and needs assessment, how to plan programs, and how to implement those programs. (Dr. Kerr's survey questionnaire is reproduced, with permission, in Appendix A.)

The council took seriously Dr. Kerr's recommendations about priority needs and ministries. He suggests five:

- *Spiritual Enrichment* (Bible study, retreats, and counseling);
- *Learning Opportunities* (personal enrichment, hobbies, and academic studies);
- *Socialization* (fellowship with peers, trips, arts and crafts, and drama);

- *Service Opportunities* (telephone and office work, home re-pairs, providing transportation, visiting, and leadership op-portunities);
- *Services Needed* (finances, health, housing, visits, and em-ployment).

Park Cities has a special concern for its shut-ins. These are classified as *homebound* (the clinically ill who live at home), the *advanced age person* (a person who is ninety or older, and likely unable to attend church regularly), and the *institutionalized* (Park Cities has members in twenty-five different long-term health fa-cilities in the Dallas area). A few are accident victims, who are immobilized for only a relatively brief time. Some are perma-nently physically handicapped, and not all of these are senior adults; regardless of age, they are kept in contact with their church.

Thus, visiting some two hundred shut-ins has high priority and this requires lots of visitors. Park Cities Baptist Church is fortu-nate: it has three hundred volunteers who are presently equipped and trained to do this work. Another thirty-five are in training.

Each shut-in is contacted at least once a month. That one monthly visit can best be described as *pastoral*; the visitor often returns during the month on a more casual, less church-related visit.

Here is what happens on one of those monthly pastoral visits. There is a sharing of personal news. There is sharing of news from the church; together they review the current church news-letter and Sunday bulletin. Then begins what is called the *teach-ing visit*. Actually, this is a kind of one-on-one Sunday school class, which was studied earlier by the "home visitors." Visitors are instructed to be conversational, to be tactile—not to be afraid of touching the roombound member, and to maintain eye con-tact. Copies of Southern Baptist materials may be left, such as the large-print publications *Mature Living* and *Open Windows*.

Gena Hestand believes deeply in these personal visits. When I asked whether the church had some sort of tape ministry, she answered "no." She doesn't think most bedridden or chairbound persons have the patience to listen to a sixty-minute or longer service. These person-to-person visits, which are tailored to the needs and abilities of the person being visited, are far more practical and effective, in her view.

I did learn that Park Cities televises its morning worship service, so homebound and hospitalized persons do have an opportunity to share in worship, if they are so inclined. I also learned that on Communion Sundays, a volunteer who is a deacon is present to share the Lord's Supper with the person who is ill or handicapped. This is a marvelous idea: as these two persons watch the distribution of the elements in the sanctuary by way of television, the hospital patient or the nursing home resident, with the deacon, partake together in what then becomes true *communion*.

Strong friendships develop from these kinds of contacts. Visitors do return at other times, to help in some way, to do an errand, or just to converse. A young women's group in the church has formed teams of four or five persons to do volunteer work and spread some joy in nursing homes.

Hestand also has a great concern for caregivers and she conducts seminars for them. These caregivers aren't just midlifers; some of them are senior adults, people over sixty-five, who themselves are still caring for an older parent or relative. A seventy-year-old is taking care of her aunt, for example. There is need to understand what is happening to them as caregivers, she feels, both emotionally and physically. Economic realities have to be faced. Helpful resources must be identified. A realistic understanding of Alzheimer's disease is needed, along with practical suggestions on how to cope.

The vast majority of Park Cities' fifteen hundred senior adults is ambulatory and active. One ninety-five-year-old man attends Sunday worship regularly and also does daily volunteer work at a nearby middle school. Baptist women have had a strong and historic interest in missions, and older Baptist women do not lose that interest. Most of these senior adults were activists before retirement, and most continue to be active in community programs, local missions, and visitation programs.

A Wednesday night prayer meeting is still held at Park Cities Church, and it remains a popular moment in time for many senior adults who are not yet fearful of being out at night in a big city. A meal precedes the prayer service. Hestand arranges a "world travelers' night" once a month following Wednesday prayer meeting. Occasionally there is a game night. Thus, Wednesday night continues to be a time of fellowship and enrichment for many older members.

Trips are also anticipated. The church owns two fifteen-passenger vans, plans to purchase a large shuttle bus, and rents city or intercity buses as needed.

Many short trips are scheduled. Two extended trips are planned each year.

The short trips are taken in and around Dallas. Many senior adults do not enjoy driving their own cars around the city. So they will take a trip downtown, do some shopping, and have lunch together. Another example: an entire new city has been built near the Dallas/Fort Worth international airport. Few of the older adults would have seen it, if they hadn't taken a short day trip to Las Colinas.

Longer trips have taken them to Palo Duro Canyon, south of Amarillo in the Texas Panhandle, where an outdoor historical drama is performed in the state park each summer. They also have journeyed to Baptist conference centers in Glorietta, New Mexico, and Ridgecrest, North Carolina. As many as 150 persons go on these trips on three rented buses. One really extended trip was a cruise to the Bahamas, led by the church's Minister of Education. Hestand says the trips provide a special kind of fellowship for these older members. These opportunities are well publicized in the monthly newsletter, published just for senior adults.

Six hundred older adults, from different Baptist churches, attended day programs last summer at the local Baptist Association's Camp Lebanon. The Association also sponsors a series of adult Bible studies in long-term health facilities—a kind of "Vacation Bible School" for nursing home residents. These kinds of activities expand fellowship and service.

Gena Hestand is employed full-time. She has a secretary. She hopes to secure funding for a part-time intern from a local seminary, someone interested in learning about gerontology and older adult ministries firsthand. There are substantial expenses for transportation and special programs. Funding comes from several budgets, but this kind of program costs approximately $60,000 a year.

I asked Gena if there were anything she would do differently, if she were just beginning her work. She didn't reply immediately, but then said she wished she had had more formal training in gerontology. In fact, she still feels the need for this, and plans to do some graduate work in the field.

I asked if she ever encountered burn-out. Her answer this time was immediate. "It gets especially bad, sometimes, after you've been working in a nursing home. That's when I cry. But I know that things will never get better until more people know personally about these kinds of situations."

She is pushing for more advocates for nursing home residents. She would like to see some kind of financial aid—something like federal scholarship aid—for the middle-class handicapped persons who do not qualify for welfare, but soon will be qualified, as they exhaust their financial resources to pay the $50-or-more-per-day costs of long-term health care.

I knew she wasn't ordained as a pastor. I asked this seminary graduate if she minded. "No, I don't have to be ordained for what I do," she said. Then she smiled. "I do a lot of pastoral ministry, anyway, you know. In fact, many of the homebound call me 'Pastor.' " Then she paused. "There are times of crisis when being ordained would help. Perhaps, one day...."

Here are several things Hestand counsels, if you contemplate beginning a ministry with senior adults in your church:

- Find another church that's doing something in adult ministries. Ask questions. Learn how they did it and do it.
- Find and read a copy of Dr. Horace L. Kerr's book *How to Minister to Senior Adults in Your Church* (Broadman Press).
- Survey your people and their needs. Do this with a team

that's been trained to do the job. If you don't need a telephone reassurance program, don't start one!

• Don't duplicate what the community is already doing. Senior adult programs are not limited to what happens in your congregation. Some of your members are members of Kiwanis and other civic clubs. Many are involved in the Retired Seniors Volunteer Program, in book and garden clubs, and other activities. Meet the unmet needs.

• Always be ready to evaluate whatever you are doing. Every program can be enhanced.

There are new things Hestand is planning. She would like to offer some college-level courses. She sees a need for respite care for caregivers. She wants to hold a seminar for widowed persons. She would like her church to employ a full-time professional counselor. She wishes that they had their own hospice program—and more multi-care housing units. And she needs that seminary intern.

For more information about this program, write: Park Cities Baptist Church, 3933 Northwest Parkway, Dallas, TX 75225.

Central Presbyterian Church
Austin, Texas

This is an inner city church which until 1984 was known as "First Southern Presbyterian Church." That says much about its sense of history and position in the community. We were members of it thirty years ago; when we returned to Austin ten years ago, we joined a church closer to our home, away from the inner city. So have many other people over the years. Central Presbyterian Church today has a preponderance of older people with a sprinkling of young couples and midlifers. Its youth group is small and reflects the membership profile of the church.

One of only four churches that remain in the inner city, Central Presbyterian is located five blocks from the state capitol and is surrounded by hotels, federal buildings, and skyscrapers. Parking in its immediate environs has disappeared. All of its members live outside that central, inner city.

I'm not suggesting that Central Presbyterian Church is dying. It shows many remarkable signs of life. Its weekday Lenten series attracts a large group of worshipers, many coming from business and government offices close by. There is a weekly noontime concert, followed by a sandwich lunch. A professional counseling center has been established. Its diminished youth group is combining resources and activities with youth groups of other churches. It maintains a strong Wednesday family night program, with a shared meal and activities for various age groups and interests. It is significant, I think, that with the possible exception of the Wednesday evening program, all of these activities reflect an intentional outreach beyond the membership of the church.

This, then, is the motivation for its *Older Persons Ministry*, now in its eleventh year, and presently directed by Edna Youngblood.

The purpose of this ministry is to provide an opportunity for growth to older adults throughout the community—a ministry that will keep minds active and involved. This is done through programs, trips, and visitation.

"Senior Tuesdays" are held on the first and third Tuesdays of each month. A chartered city transit bus makes stops at two retirement centers, located on the fringes of the inner city, to bring participants to the church. Volunteer drivers use their own vehicles to bring others who use walkers and wheelchairs. Forty to fifty-five people participate in the program, which includes both members and nonmembers of the church.

A brief worship service begins at 12:05 noon, followed by lunch. The activities program begins at 1:15 P.M. and concludes one hour later. (It should be mentioned that Central Presbyterian is barrier-free; it has both an elevator and a motorized chair-incline over one set of stairs.)

There are two choices for after-lunch activity: bingo or a book review with discussion. Edna Youngblood has tried to introduce other group games, but bingo is still the more popular of the two alternatives.

Another component of the church's program is the "Over Sixty

Group," which plans events away from the church campus. There are excursions to restaurants or cafeterias, also held twice a month, alternating between lunch or dinner. A tour is scheduled six times a year; occasionally these are overnight.

A recent tour took the group by chartered bus to Kerrville, about 120 miles southwest of Austin in the hill country. The group visited the Western Museum, a purse factory, and the Avery silversmiths. They had lunch at the Inn of the Hills.

About forty people participate in the Over Sixty Group. Not all of them are members of Central Presbyterian. Some also come from University United Methodist Church, where Edna Youngblood is a member.

Edna makes two points about these activities.

"This isn't *entertainment*," she says. These older adults secure their entertainment in other ways. What it is is *socialization*—a chance to relax and visit with friends. Edna says that older adults just don't go visiting as much as they used to. Some have given up their cars. Others don't like to drive in big city traffic, especially at night. They live more isolated lives than before, but the church is helping them to recapture the blessing of friendship.

"Second, this isn't *extravagant*," Edna affirms. Eating out and traveling can be expensive, she admits, and many of Central's older members are comfortably affluent and can afford just about anything. "But others in the group live on modest, fixed incomes," she adds. Thus costs for these various events are kept low by design, often below actual cost, in order that more people will be able to participate. Edna includes line items in her budget for transportation and contingencies, which help to subsidize these activities for persons less able to afford them.

Volunteer drivers bring a dozen or more persons to worship service on Sunday; these persons are older adults without transportation or who are handicapped. A newly acquired van will facilitate this part of Central's ministry. Edna Youngblood makes this observation, however: she has discovered that most of the older adults cannot sit through a Sunday school class and morning worship service. She wants to schedule transportation so that the older adults can choose one or the other.

Visitation is the other ingredient of this Older Persons Ministry.
More than a dozen volunteers work with Edna in special programs for homebound or roombound members. One volunteer
sends holiday greeting and birthday cards. Others prepare holiday decorations for the homes or rooms of shut-ins. There is a
mobile library, bringing books and magazines to homes and nursing homes—a significant service, now that the city library has discontinued its bookmobile operation. Elders and deacons of the
church visit the homebound regularly.

Central Presbyterian chose to have a tape ministry. It provides
each homebound person with a simple-to-operate audio tape
cassette playback unit (only one lever turns it on or off). Tape
cassettes of the morning worship service are delivered to each
homebound person and later picked up for recycling.

For those persons physically unable to attend the Tuesday
luncheons, an annual *homebound luncheon* is held at the
church. Every effort is made to bring as many handicapped or
disabled persons as possible.

As is the case with Pat Baker, Edna Youngblood is also a part-
time coordinator. In her words, she is "paid for twenty hours a
week," but she usually works more hours than that. She also administers a volunteer program in her own church called *Care
Corps* (see description in Chapter 7). Her annual budget is
$6,000, excluding salary. Her work and program are determined
by an Older Persons Task Force, representing participants and
volunteer workers. The task force is accountable to the "Serving
Ministry Committee" of the Session. Her counsel to others is to
begin simply and not duplicate what other activity centers are
doing. She hopes to involve more downtown churches, so that
more things can be done together for more older adults.

For more information, write: Central Presbyterian Church,
200 E. Eighth St., Austin, TX 78701.

Saint John's Evangelical Lutheran Church
San Antonio, Texas

Carolyn and I heard music—live music with a hefty beat—as

we entered Saint John's Activity Center. It was just after ten o'clock in the morning and about twenty people had already arrived. In fact, some of them were already dancing! This happened to be the one day in the month that featured live music and, obviously, it was a popular day. The combo musicians were all past sixty, and they played music from the forties, and played it joyously. Before the hot lunch was served, probably fifty people had arrived. Some came on their own. Others were brought in the church van.

The Activity Center began seven years ago as an outreach ministry to the many elderly people who lived in the vicinity. From that beginning emerged a new organization called *Christian Senior Service Providers*, sponsored by both Saint John's and Grace Lutheran churches. Its full-time executive director is Howard Schuetze, a former school teacher, who has been with the program for three years.

The two churches are separated by a mile and a half; both are located in the central city. Grace Church is near an interstate exit, on the northeastern boundary of the downtown area. Saint John's, known as the "Lutheran Cathedral of the Southwest," is on its southern boundary, just south of La Villita, a reconstruction of a tiny Mexican village, and due west of the site of the 1968 Hemisfair. The Alamo is within walking distance of both churches. Museums, a concert hall, a sports arena, and a convention center are close-by. There is a lot of activity in the neighborhood.

That activity, however, rarely touches the lives of most of the elderly persons who live in the area. Their income is limited. Many are frail. Thus, Christian Senior Service Providers has chosen to reach out in several ways, and it affects the lives of several hundred people every day.

There is the Activity Center with its weekday congregate meal program at Saint John's (and the monthly swing session). It is open mornings through lunch. At Grace Lutheran, you'll find "Grace Place," a new senior adult day care center, one of six in San Antonio. It is open from 7:30 A.M. until 6 P.M., Monday through Friday.

There is a diverse meal program. Sixty to seventy meals are served daily in each center. Another one hundred meals are prepared for direct delivery to homes, distributed through several satellite nutrition sites. Two vans and a hatchback deliver the Meals on Wheels.

The program requires dozens of volunteers, but there are ten paid staff people to help carry out this extensive ministry. Its annual budget is about $300,000.

The two churches provide 40 percent of this amount, some of this through contributions of space and services. Some of the money comes from client fees. (Suggested price for lunch is $1.75; Grace Place charges $12 a day, which includes the hot lunch.) The rest of the money comes from federal sources, the city's general fund, and United Way.

Howard Schuetze knows that that $300,000 figure will frighten many people who would like to begin a similar program. He is quick to remind anyone that this huge program began seven years ago with a rather modest grant of $7,000 from the Lutheran Church in America. He emphasizes that programs can grow gradually.

Schuetze has several hopes for the future.

He would like more of the downtown churches to participate and share in this program.

He wants to establish more adult day care centers. He thinks these should be located within the four quadrants of this million-plus metropolis. In his view, they should be located closer to where caregivers live and work.

He wants to see more support groups. Counseling is needed for both clients and caregivers.

Schuetze emphasizes and counsels the greatest possible consultation with parish leaders and membership. The program began with their knowledge, concurrence, and support. As the program grew and its outreach expanded, the parish went along but no longer occupied the decision-making position it once held. Schuetze believes it is important that the congregation not feel left out, that its ownership be preserved and nourished.

There is need, also, for interpretation to the parish. Outreach programs are of primary help to the poor, many of whom live on welfare. Howard Schuetze believes that a strong antiwelfare feeling, caused by bias and misinformation, permeates our society. Clearly, ongoing conversation with constituent supporters is essential.

For further information about this program, write: Christian Senior Service Providers, 502 E. Nueva, San Antonio, TX 78205.

We have looked at four church-related programs, with different approaches, different programs, and different price tags. Now what do we do?

Next Steps

1. Begin by making your church or temple barrier free, accessible to the handicapped. You need to do this if you plan any kind of ministry to older persons; you ought to do this for your present ongoing program. This requires the construction of at least one ramp—more if there are several levels in your building. Grab bars in rest rooms need to be installed. Rest room doors may require widening or repositioning. Try getting in and out of a rest room with a wheelchair! (A five-foot turning radius is recommended.) Consult with a local architect or with your state board of building standards.

2. Assess your needs. Interview the older adults in your congregation. A census of your neighborhood (or "larger parish") will provide the hard data necessary for careful planning and decision-making.

3. Learn what other churches are doing in your city in special senior adult ministries. Benefit and learn from their experience.

4. Read *How to Minister to Senior Adults in Your Church* by Horace L. Kerr (Broadman Press). Another helpful guide is *Aging Persons In The Community Of Faith* by Donald F. Clingan (Christian Board of Publication, Box 179, St. Louis, MO 63166).

5. Review chapters 1, 4, 6, 9, and peruse 12. These all have

implications for planning for senior adult ministries.

6. Learn how your denomination can help you in planning and training. Most church bodies have offices on aging, with many resources and resource persons. Check with your pastor or your judicatory office (diocese, presbytery, conference, association, etc.). You may already have this information from the initial survey of your community and available resources (refer to Chapter 1).

7. Include persons from the broad spectrum of your congregational membership as you plan. Older adults must be included, since this will be their program. Key leaders should also be consulted, since they will have a say in ultimate decision-making and funding.

8. Hire a coordinator, even if this person works only a few hours each week. You need someone with a commitment to the church. You also need someone with a knowledge of gerontology, perhaps with experience in social work or health care. Volunteers are needed and helpful. But a caring, knowledgeable, and responsible person needs to be in charge.

9. If you've decided the time is not yet right for beginning a program, consider offering a scholarship to someone who is seeking more expertise in the field of working with older adults. This might be arranged through a seminary or church-related college. It is significant, I think, that the people in charge in the preceding four example programs all happen to be laypersons. There aren't enough trained people in this field to fill the positions which will open up within the next five years. Whether you are a layperson or clergy, perhaps you yourself can help meet that future need.

10. Consider the "Shepherd's Center" concept as an approach for a special ministry to (and with!) older adults in your congregation. It is discussed in Chapter 12.

11

Giving and Receiving
Support Systems for Care-Sharing

During the past several decades we have learned how important support groups can be in dealing with a commonly shared problem. Alcoholics Anonymous is probably the best known, from which have sprung AL-ANON (for the nonalcoholic family member) and Alateen (for children of alcoholic parents). Parents of mentally retarded children have formed groups. A more recent support group is Parents Anonymous, for persons who have abused their children and want to stop. Many churches have discovered that support groups are a significant way of sharing faith and love.

Support groups for older persons and caregivers have been established around some physical need, usually a disease or some continuing medical problem. Exceptions are such advocacy groups as AARP (American Association of Retired Persons) and the Gray Panthers.

Medical-problem support groups include: *Alzheimer's Disease and Related Disorders Association, arthritis* and *stroke clubs, Crohn's and Ulcerative Colitis, Mended Hearts* (for heart disorders), and other clusters of people concerned about cancer, diabetes, and Parkinson's disease. Meetings feature speakers, films, and information about new developments. But the most important ingredient of such gatherings is sharing. Both care receiver and caregiver find the opportunity to ventilate frustrations and to learn from each other how better to cope with accidents, illness, and disabilities. This need is particularly acute for families living with such memory-loss diseases as Alzheimer's or Parkinson's.

They need to know what is reversible and what is not. They need affirmation, particularly when home care is no longer possible.

Saint Albans' Stroke Club

An example of an impairment support group is a stroke club organized at the Veterans Administration Extended Care Center in Saint Albans, New York. It was initiated by the center's Speech Pathology and Audiology Service.

The club provides opportunities for socialization and group interaction to a large number of veterans with speech and language disabilities. Most have multiple handicaps and are wheelchair bound. Families and friends of the patients are invited. While not a therapy group, professional hospital staff persons participate from time to time—persons such as the hospital chief of staff, speech pathologist, audiologist, psychologist, social worker, occupational therapist, and chaplain.

Various activities are offered: a current events discussion group, games, yoga and other exercises, a lending library of publications dealing with stroke, and counseling for spouses, families, and friends. An attempt was made to organize a glee club. For the most part, patients chose not to participate in these activities.

However, as many as thirty persons regularly attend the meetings and apparently enjoy the discussions. Few of the patients are able to initiate a conversation, but the leaders feel that communication has improved both inside and outside of the group. Topics discussed have been how to maintain emotional stability, inability to return to work, death and dying, and the difficulty of initiating new friendships and keeping old ones. Veterans' interest in politics was sparked by the visit of two New York candidates for the U.S. Senate.

For information about this program, write: Speech Pathology and Audiology Service, Veterans Administration Extended Care Center, Saint Albans, NY 11425.

National Organizational Contacts

As you assess the needs of older persons in your community, check to see if support groups exist to meet these needs. If not, getting one of them started would be a tremendous service.

There may be local organizations you can contact. If not, here are addresses of a few national groups to whom you could write for information on how to start a support group in your locality.

Alzheimer's Disease and Related Disorders Association, 360 N. Michigan Ave., Suite 601, Chicago, IL 60601.

American Cancer Society, 219 E. 42d St., New York, NY 10021.

American Diabetes Association, 18 E. 48th St., New York, NY 10017.

American Heart Association, 44 W. 23d St., New York, NY 10010.

National Arthritis Foundation, 1314 Spring St., NW, Atlanta, GA 30309.

Divorce

Older persons are affected by divorce as much as younger persons. Some are themselves involved in the process of divorce. A larger number of persons are affected by the divorce of their children. Both groups need support systems to carry them through this time of difficulty and bewilderment.

Older women are most affected by divorce in later life. The stories about older men who search for fading youth with a new, younger companion are all too true. Wives are discarded and abandoned, often left without resources. In such cases, wives may need to initiate divorce proceedings, if they are to survive financially in their later years. Because of cultural and religious upbringing, many older women are reluctant to take what they perceive to be a drastic step. Military wives suffer their own kind of injustice, as they lose medical and commissary benefits even when there has been a formal divorce. These persons desperately need a group that can provide both support and professional counseling.

Such a group is called "Divorce After Sixty" and additional information can be secured from the Turner Geriatric Clinic, University of Michigan Hospitals, 1010 Wall St., Ann Arbor, MI 48105.

The second aspect of divorce—when children are divorced—is just beginning to be researched. The Department of Psychological Sciences of Purdue University completed a survey in 1983 of 141 adult children who had experienced "marital disruption" (divorce, death of a spouse, and/or remarriage) whose parents were over sixty years of age.

A key finding was related to dollars. Children who had experienced marital disruption were financially less well off, and they were less willing to support elderly parents. In fact, 84 percent felt "there was a point beyond which they could not continue to help their parents. If helping parents threatened their job or meant denying their own children, then such relationships could not continue."

Another finding is concerned with communication. The report observes: "Although relationships between parents and adult children were not necessarily worse because of marital disruption, interviewers found that adult children with marital disruption had weaker perception of the extent of their aging parents' needs—a result, in many cases, of reduced communication."

A third aspect, not addressed by the Indiana survey, is associated with grandparenting. The rights of grandparents are just beginning to be reviewed by the courts. Even though forty-two states have enacted laws regarding "grandparent rights," the reality is that grandparents are often denied access and visitation rights to grandchildren where there has been a divorce, especially when a custody fight has been nasty. I happen to believe that an intergenerational connection is vital, especially within disintegrating families. Grandchildren need grandparents, and grandparents need grandchildren, for the ultimate good of the grandchildren.

These are issues that can be upsetting to older adults at a time in their lives when they hope for more stable relationships with children and grandchildren. I do not know of specific support groups that exist to help older parents through this trauma. Perhaps we need a Grandparents Anonymous.

Bereavement

Another need for a support system takes place when a loved one dies. Many churches have bereavement or grief-sharing groups. There is a need for more of them. Parents whose young children die, parents of older children who died from terminal illness or who were killed or who killed themselves—these parents suffer deeply and many would benefit if they could share their grief.

The older person who loses a spouse also needs loving support, perhaps over an extended period of time. An older friend told me several months after his wife's death, "I never knew how much I would miss my mate." Such persons need someone to talk to, about death and dying—and living.

Caregivers

Children who care for their parents, or some other disabled or sick loved one, are called the *sandwich generation*. Their own children are grown; and just as they begin to look forward to more time for leisure and freedom, they are often required to become parents to their parents. They are caught in the middle.

Sudden caregiving is one of the most serious of many midlife crises. Carolyn and I know the feeling quite well. My earlier book, *A Guide to Caring for and Coping With Aging Parents*, was the result of our decade of experience. And we so often wished for a support group where we could unburden ourselves and where we could learn from others.

The University of Michigan, through its Institute of Gerontology (Ann Arbor, MI 48105), offers a six-session program called "As Parents Grow Older." This is a good beginning and many groups, formed during the course, decide to continue.

A trained group leader encourages a nonjudgmental and accepting environment. Participants are free to identify with each other's problems and to express their feelings openly. This is a place for venting anger, frustration, and hostility. Trust of and for each other must emerge. And the group must be able to go beyond expressing feelings to dealing positively with those feelings. Resources and ideas are exchanged.

The group is limited to fifteen persons. Some drop out because of the death of a loved one. Some drop out and return. New members are always welcomed because they lend their support by sharing new experiences. The group meets in a senior citizen center, which provides a setting where information about various community activities for the aging is shared.

What kinds of problems and issues emerge? A daughter cares for her bedridden mother twenty-four hours a day. She needs additional help, but can't afford it. More importantly, she needs respite care herself, time to take a recess from her intense caregiving. A son resents the extended presence of his semi-invalid mother in his large family; he learns to be free to talk with her about his feelings and discovers that his mother would prefer another arrangement. Children are often angry that siblings do not share the burden of caregiving. And often a confused parent with severe memory loss will somehow fondly recall and recite the virtues of an absent child, who may be dead or may never have shared in the parent's care. These are hard, emotionally upsetting issues. A support group can be very helpful where these kinds of problems can be raised and, perhaps, solved or resolved.

An organization has been formed to foster this kind of group-help. It is called the National Support Center for Families of the Aging. Its purpose is (1) to help family members cope with their responsibility to older relatives and (2) to help individuals come to terms with their own aging process.

The organization publishes materials to help professionals and laypersons. Its manual, *Help for Families of the Aging*, prepared for small-group seminars, is very helpful. This organization offers support to individuals, particularly through its referral program, putting aching caregivers in touch with fellow pilgrims. It educates the general public about the needs of caregivers.

For more information, write: National Support Center for Families of the Aging, Box 245, Swarthmore, PA 19081.

Individual Support Systems

We have been discussing group approaches to sharing and solving common problems. Such groups are, indeed, important support systems for care receivers and caregivers. But there is also a need for individuals to assume certain support functions on behalf of others. Communities can help this happen by identifying needs of older people and creating some way or mechanism for linking persons with persons.

Many older people need a trustworthy person to manage their affairs. Not all of them live in nursing homes, although many do. These elderly folk may need a "representative payee" to handle their social security benefits. They may even need a guardian, although the court is the determining voice. Or the need may be for an unofficial ombudsman, someone who runs interference with government agencies, creditors, and sometimes even family members.

The individual doesn't have to do everything himself. The situation may require the professional services of a trust department of a respected local bank. It does mean that some reliable person will assume whatever responsibility is necessary for the well-being of a handicapped, confused, or otherwise incapacitated person.

This is something like the "big brother" or "big sister" approach, except that an *older* person is being helped to live more securely and happily. It is a one-to-one relationship, when there isn't anyone else who can be a true and honest friend. In a way, it is like adopting a parent, an uncle, or an aunt—and being a loving substitute son, daughter, nephew, or niece.

A group that has dealt with this need, particularly in nursing homes, is the Task Force on Aging Persons of Metro Ministries, Austin, Texas. Its address is 100 E. 27th St., Austin, TX 78705.

Part Four

Meeting Basic Esteem Needs

12

Achievement
The Shepherd's Center Concept

A Shepherd's Center is a senior center, but with a vast difference. Its specific goal is to meet the *esteem* needs of older adults. Dr. Elbert C. Cole, senior pastor of Kansas City's Central United Methodist Church, who is as close to being the founder of the Shepherd Center movement as anybody, describes it as "empowerment of older adults." Senior centers are mostly run by paid staff, usually young staff. In contrast, the Shepherd's Center "links older adults together in conceiving, planning, making decisions, and doing services and programs that help some to survive and others to find meaning for their lives." More than sixty Shepherd's Centers, scattered across this nation and Canada, uniquely meet adult needs for esteem of others and self, for independence and achievement.

The concept of a Shepherd's Center, then, is "creative self-help support." It is both self-help and shared ownership of a program.

At the age of ninety, Samuel Curtis Reaves directs *Shepherd's Centers, International*, a training organization that helps others begin similar programs. Sam has had a cataract operation and wears a hearing aid, but I would wager that his mind is as alert as it ever was. He always wanted to be a school teacher, and his first job was teacher-principal of a two-room school in Braggadocio (yes, there is such a town!), Missouri. Eventually he became a superintendent of schools, then an administrative officer of the Boy Scouts of America and the American Heart Association. He was business administrator of the Central United Methodist

159

Church in Kansas City when its pastor, Dr. Cole, first envisaged what would become the first Shepherd's Center.

A group of five men from the church began to deliver meals to seven homebound women in January of 1972. Their experience identified two needs: first, they were amazed at how many small repairs were needed in the homes they visited. Second, they learned that most of the women needed transportation, since they had never learned to drive and were unable to use public transit. Within six months, a repair service and transportation program were in place. Dr. Cole described what had happened in his congregation to his local ministers' alliance. That was the beginning. Other churches and synagogues wanted to share in what was then a totally new approach to outreach ministries for older persons.

The group limited its service to a part of Kansas City that had a population of fifty-three thousand. The original Shepherd's Center still operates in the same geographical area, where the senior population has now doubled within a decade (from 11 percent to 22.1 percent). A task force petitioned the state of Missouri for a charter, choosing the name *Shepherd's Center*, based on the first phrase of the Twenty-third Psalm. Early funding came from the Hallmark Foundation.

At that time, just a dozen years ago, not a single college or seminary in the Kansas City area offered a course in gerontology. Today, all of them offer such courses and most of them include Shepherd's Centers as learning projects for their interns.

Since 1972, the program has grown to five centers in Kansas City and sixty-two throughout North America (there is now a Shepherd's Center in Canada). They are located in a variety of places and buildings. Former mansions are used, but so are store-front locations in inner city ghettos. Most are located in cities, but there are several in rural locations. One Shepherd's Center has been organized on an Indian reservation. (Addresses of these centers may be found in Appendix D.)

The expansion of the program is due to the work of Sam Reaves, whom we've already met, and Dr. Paul B. Maves. Dr. Maves is a Methodist clergyman, a former retirement-home administrator, and director of the Shepherd's Centers International training program. He is an author of several books on aging, and his *Older Volunteers in Church and Community* (Judson Press) and *A Place to Live in Your Later Years* (Augsburg) are especially helpful.

Dr. Maves says the Shepherd's Center is a new twist on an old idea. "The old idea is that of the senior center. The new twist is fourfold," he explains. "First, older people themselves should bear primary responsibility for caring for each other. Second, older people themselves should control the planning, implement the program, and own the organization by contributing to its cost. Third, delivery of services to the home should be central, thus preventing premature and inappropriate institutionalization. Finally, the center should not be a place to which persons come, so much as it is a presence in the neighborhood or an expression of the pastoral care of the congregations." Dr. Maves puts it in theological terms: "This is a commitment to the creation of a *covenant community*, in which persons care for each other because they care about each other."

Sam Reaves has strong convictions about how older people can control the planning. The majority of the governing board must be sixty-five years old or older. New people with new ideas are constantly needed. Thus board members serve two-year terms in three rotating classes. A coordinating council, made up of volunteers, develops a program and seeks approval from the governing board. Finding new committee members is no problem, says Sam. "We have people knocking on the door, wanting to help." The Kansas City program at any given time has between four hundred and five hundred volunteers eager to help and work!

The services provided by a Shepherd's Center are similar to many other programs. However, the services are clustered in a different way, and they are part of a single project, which is primarily staffed and organized by senior citizens themselves.

The services are described as:

- *Life maintenance.* These are services that help people to survive, such as Meals on Wheels, home health services, home repair, employment, and companion aides.

- *Life enrichment.* These are programs in adult education, volunteer service, health education, and advocacy. They also include support groups.
- *Life reconstruction.* This is an area that deals with retirement, widowhood, alcohol recovery, and mental health concerns.
- *Life celebration.* These are gatherings and events that give meaning and purpose to life.

The programs vary between centers, but each Shepherd's Center gives emphasis to these four levels of activity: life maintenance, enrichment, reconstruction, and celebration.

Here are a couple of examples of how the process works. On the day I visited the Shepherd's Center in Kansas City, a group of volunteers, called the Gadabouts, were touring a Rotary Club campsite at Lake Jacomo. They felt there was a need for a scheduled camping program for older adults; but they wanted to check out the site to determine logistics, number of volunteers required, and what kind of extra funding would be needed.

Another example: the Handyman Program. Upon request, retired skilled workmen make minor repairs—electrical, plumbing, carpentry, and painting. All handymen are registered with the center and each provides his own tools and transportation. Each is paid $5 an hour, directly to the workman; materials are reimbursed at cost. The fee enhances a retiree's income; it also provides skilled and inexpensive repairs to the homeowner or renter. A coordinator keeps card index files up-to-date. Volunteers handle telephone requests and contact the appropriate skilled worker.

Dr. Maves, the director of training, offers a checklist for starting a Shepherd's Center.

1. Start talking to people about their interests, needs, and skills. Talk to all kinds of people—old, young, and middle-aged.

2. Convene a meeting of interested persons; be sure that older persons are included and have an opportunity to be the major decision-makers.

3. If there is sufficient interest and agreement, organize a task

force to make a more careful study of the situation. It can determine where older persons live, what they need, and what resources are already available.

4. Following your task force report, establish a more formal organization with a board of directors. If you are going to solicit and expend funds, secure nonprofit, tax-exempt corporation status.

5. Limit the geographical area you intend to serve. Distances and numbers of persons to be helped must be manageable. Political subdivisions, census tracts, or natural neighborhoods will help define the boundaries of your service area.

6. Begin by meeting a priority need. "Don't try too much at one time," counsels Dr. Maves. "Don't deal with problems that are beyond your resources or that may be inappropriate for a group on the local level. Once you establish a program and it is working, then you may be able and ready to tackle something else." He reminds us how the Kansas City program began—with five men delivering meals to seven women. Other programs began as visitation or telephone reassurance projects.

7. Once you have identified that single priority need and know ways to meet it and pay for it, secure a coordinator. Each program should have a separate volunteer coordinator or supervisor. Coordinators, in turn, recruit the volunteers who will work with them.

Sam Reaves admits that many similar programs have emerged over the years, but he still believes that the Shepherd's Center concept is worth exploring. He highly recommends participating in one of five four-day training events, held annually in Kansas City, with additional on-site consultation as needed.

Sam likes to limit groups to no more than fifteen people, representing both clergy and laity. Cost of the seminar in early 1985 was $160. This includes four days of workshops and four meals. (It does not include transportation or lodging, but the center often arranges inexpensive housing through local cooperating congregations.)

This is the place for novices to learn about recruitment of volunteers and funding. More importantly, the seminar gives guidance in need assessment of the community, planning, and administration. It emphasizes a positive image of aging and clarification of feelings about getting older and about working with older people. And, of course, the seminar deals with the Shepherd's Center concept and philosophy. I believe that anyone interested in any kind of program for older adults could benefit from participation in one of these seminars.

For information about these seminars, write: Shepherd's Centers International, 5218 Oak St., Kansas City, MO 64112.

Chandler Center

Shepherd's Centers are known by other names. One of these is Chandler Center in San Antonio, Texas. It is adjacent to Chandler Memorial Home—both an apartment complex for retirees and a long-term health facility—and is related to Morningside Manor, sponsored by the Episcopal Diocese of West Texas, the Southwest Conference of the United Methodist Church, and First Presbyterian Church of San Antonio.

Chandler Center is located in the historic Chandler House, a beautiful old mansion in the Monte Vista Historical District of San Antonio, built in the late 1800s. In 1923 it was incorporated to serve "aged gentlewomen in their declining years." In 1975 it became part of the Morningside Manor complex of facilities for older persons.

Nearly four thousand people are members of Chandler House. Services are free but most contribute the suggested $25 annual membership donation. As many as eighteen hundred lunches are served each month (for which a separate charge is made). Paid staff are conspicuous by their absence. There are a director, kitchen help, and support people from the Chandler Memorial Home. Older volunteers are very much in evidence— at the reception desk, answering the telephone, teaching, serving, and planning.

I am looking at a typical calendar for October, 1984. Activities are scheduled every morning, Monday through Friday, with some events carried over into the afternoons. The AARP board uses this facility for its meetings. There are classes in photography, yoga, German, Spanish, oil and watercolor painting, and square dancing. There are travelogs, bridge games, book reviews, a special group called "SHHH" for the hard-of-hearing, sessions for knitting and crocheting, and a Shakespeare Club. On Fridays, there is blood pressure screening. Anyone with a birthday celebrates on the third Friday afternoon of the month.

Extra events during October included a men's breakfast with a special speaker from the Texas Highway Department. A flea market was held on the huge front porch of the mansion on Halloween. And a monthly potluck supper was held on a Sunday afternoon for Chandler Center members, families, and guests.

Home services are provided, which include not only home repairs but also laundry and housekeeping services. These are coordinated by older adult volunteers at the center, but the services are actually provided by staff support and maintenance people from the Chandler Memorial Home. Charges are minimal and determined by the Chandler Home.

Outreach services include Meals on Wheels, transportation to medical appointments and grocery shopping, and an information referral system. A food co-op sells fresh vegetables from San Antonio's Farmers' Market. A new Community Health Service is planned.

For information about this particular "Shepherd's Center," write: Chandler Center, 137 W. French Place, San Antonio, TX 78212.

Next Steps

Religious communities are the ideal entities to begin programs such as Shepherd's Centers. Dr. Paul Maves thinks that religious congregations may well be the only groups ready with sufficient resources to assume this responsibility. The New Federalism, with its cutbacks in federal spending and emphasis on locally governed and funded programs, offers a special challenge to churches and synagogues.

Dr. Maves is also concerned that affluent communities and churches look beyond their own needs and be ready to share leadership, experience, and money with those communities that do not enjoy similar resources. He thinks that more thought should be given to the quality of life, as well as to the quantity of programs we design for older people. Issues of social justice are not usually discussed within the context of gerontology, but how we deal with the poor and the vulnerable are issues that affect the expectations of our aging neighbors.

Shepherd's Centers, by whatever name they are known, are forums where older persons can discuss and affirm the priorities of government, at all levels, which will determine whether the last third of life will be worth living. They are also places where older persons are deciding, now, how they can best live out their lives.

13

Outreach
Helping Others and Each Other

Most older people are ready, willing, and able to help others. Sometimes the task for community leaders seeking compassionate alternatives for older persons is often as simple as putting these older persons in touch with existing programs. If programs are not available in a particular area, then opportunities for involvement must be developed.

Government Programs

Begin by checking the government blue or business white pages of your telephone directory to learn whether certain federal programs are active in your community.

ACTION is the umbrella name under which several volunteer programs function. It is an independent agency established by executive order of President Lyndon Johnson.

ACTION administers:

- *RSVP* (Retired Senior Volunteer Program). Some 300,000 older Americans have discovered opportunities for service in hundreds of local voluntary agencies through RSVP.
- *Senior Companions* is a relatively new program designed to provide help to the frail elderly.
- The *Foster Grandparents* program provides opportunities for older persons to care for young children.
- *VISTA* (Volunteers In Service To America) is a domestic "Peace Corps" program, which recruits persons from all age groups, including retirees. If you cannot locate a local

ACTION office and would like more information, write ACTION, 806 Connecticut Ave., NW, Washington, DC 20525.

Another independent agency of the federal government is the Small Business Administration, which offers qualified older persons a special opportunity to serve in *SCORE*. The letters stand for *Senior Corps of Retired Business Executives.* Retired businessmen, accountants, manufacturers, bankers, and other executives volunteer their time to help new small business entrepreneurs get started. They participate in workshops and in individual consultations.

For detailed information about SCORE, contact your local SBA office or write: Small Business Administration, 1441 L St., NW, Washington, DC 20416.

One other federal source is the *Operation Mainstream* program, administered by the Forest Service of the U.S. Department of Agriculture. The program operates in twenty states and employs older persons for beautification and conservation projects on an average of three days a week. For information, write: USDA Forest Service, Room 3234 South, Agriculture Building, 12th and Independence Ave., SW, Washington, DC 20250.

Another outdoor conservation and beautification program is *Green Thumb*, sponsored by the National Farmers Union. It seeks applicants with a farming background to work part-time in programs in twenty-four states. For information, write: Green Thumb, Inc., 1012 14th St., NW, Washington, DC 20005.

Other Employment Opportunities

The Austin Parks and Recreation Department provides three opportunities for older persons to be employed and be of help to the community.

The *Senior Aides Program* is a community service employment program for older persons. A limited number of persons fifty-five years old or older, who meet low-income eligibility requirements, are employed in nonprofit agencies throughout the city. Many are employed in senior centers or adult day care centers.

Experience Unlimited is a telephone referral system, which puts people of any age who need work done in touch with people of fifty years and above who are interested and qualified to do the kind of work that is requested. Most requests are for babysitters, companions, and skilled workmen. This is not a volunteer program: people are paid for their work.

Babysitters are most often asked to go to the client's home. However, there are increasing requests for an older person to pick up children at school and keep them for a few hours in the older person's home until the parent can pick them up.

There is usually a shortage of people who will do light work around the house, since most requests are for live-in companions. Such care requires some light housekeeping, meal preparation, and personal assistance for the elderly person.

Plumbers, carpenters, electricians, and painters are always in great demand.

The Old Bakery and Emporium is housed in a historic building, which was once a bakery, located across the street from the Texas State Capitol. In its coffee shop the Old Bakery offers home-baked breads and pastries prepared by seniors. The Emporium sells handicrafts made by older adults. A hospitality desk welcomes visitors and gives them tourist information. The facility provides people over fifty with a way to supplement their income, as well as volunteer opportunities for persons of any age.

For information about any of these three programs, write Austin Parks and Recreation Department, Senior Programs, 403 E. 15th St., Austin, TX 78701.

Information about the Senior Community Aides Program may also be secured from the National Council on the Aging, Inc., 600 Maryland Ave., SW, West Wing 100, Washington, DC 20024.

Persons interested in marketing handicrafts should contact the Handicrafts Marketing Sales, Inc., 1001 Connecticut Ave., NW, Washington, DC 20036.

Intergenerational Caregiving

This California-based program began in 1979. It grew out of

an awareness of the increasing number of working mothers and the fact that today's mobile nuclear family, often headed by a single parent, rarely includes an older adult, which in an earlier time was usually a grandparent.

The organizing group was the Department of Family Health Care Nursing of the University of California in San Francisco. The organizers believed that children lose much from the absence of a grandparent. Grandparents traditionally offer children individual attention and interest, unhurried help, a sense of security and roots, and understanding.

The organizers of the California program wanted to fill the gap but felt that older persons would benefit from exposure to recent insights of early childhood development. What emerged was a childhood development course followed by a supervised caregiving internship. Class and practical work became a twenty-nine week experience and led to placement as volunteer or paid staff in a child care facility.

The project demonstrated that such intergenerational caregiving benefited both children and adults. Organizers tell stories similar to the experience of my wife, Carolyn. She directed a children's day care center in Elkhart, Indiana, and one of her favorite and most helpful volunteers was a grandfather, who visited once a week. He would tell an occasional story, but mostly he came to be a substitute father and grandfather, which was very important for the children who had no fathers at home. He would roughhouse with the boys. He helped all of the children to make things with tools. Just learning to drive a nail into a piece of wood became an achievement. A bird feeder to take home was a masterpiece!

Some children with little contact with older people are often frightened or repelled by the aging process; interaction with older persons soon dispelled fears and misconceptions.

Older persons had the opportunity to examine new ideas about childhood development as well as to share the wisdom of their life experience. They established warm friendships, became aware of new community resources for their own participation, and certainly discovered that they were needed.

The program was initially funded by the California State Department of Postsecondary Education. It presently receives financial support from a family foundation, the San Francisco Community College, and several community organizations.

For further information, write: Intergenerational Caregiving Program, Department of Family Health Care Nursing, University of California, San Francisco, CA 94143.

A somewhat different program is the Grandparent Aide program in Appleton, Wisconsin, which involves a commitment to be a substitute grandparent for troubled children or children with single parents. It is not baby-sitting and it goes a step beyond foster grandparent programs. It means helping the child with schoolwork, shopping, sharing a movie, talking, building traditions, and being an older friend. Training and supervision are provided by the city's social services department.

Hospital Care

Pediatric ward nurses have long known that an infant needs the physical contact of an adult holding it while it takes its bottle. There is also a need for someone to bring a meal to a child in bed and make certain that he or she actually eats it. Milk alone will not help an infant develop into an emotionally sound child or adult. Food without the stimulation of a caring adult presence and conversation will not help heal the child. The nursing staff is busy with so many things that personalized attention is a luxury few infants and children enjoy. But volunteer grandparents can provide that personalized attention; they can make a difference.

A New York State hospital and school for the mentally retarded houses 6,200 patients, of which 1,400 are children under five years of age. A typical ward holds sixty to seventy children and, on the average, three attendants are assigned to each ward. The supervisor of volunteers sought older surrogate grandparents to help. These are a few of the things older volunteers found they could do:

- Read stories to the children in the wards.
- Distribute books and magazines.
- Take groups of ambulatory children to the commissary and refreshment shop.

- Feed the children who could not feed themselves. Bottle feed the infants.
- Assist with physical therapy. Exercise the physically handicapped.
- Escort children to the various hospital services; wait with them and for them.
- Teach and lead group dancing or singing.
- Visit informally with the children. Play a game with them.
- Teach simple subject matter to children who do not attend school; help to improve their reading skills.

It is estimated that 75 percent of these children may be institutionalized for life. They have few visitors. Some, especially from the 25 percent for whom there is more hope, will benefit from individual attention and simple schoolwork. Some may be able to lead normal lives in the community, and older persons can help them.

Check with volunteer coordinators at local hospitals and other health care institutions to learn what special programs are now in place for older volunteers, or what kinds of programs might be developed.

Peer Counseling

Too often, programs for the elderly are forced to concentrate on meeting physical needs and simply do not have the time to deal with the emotional needs and problems of their clients. And older persons do need help emotionally.

A spouse dies. Someone is evicted from a mobile home community. Another faces some kind of physical disability, which creates severe depression. The elderly face their own kinds of pressures and stresses that cry out for counseling help. Institutionalization may result if these pressures and stresses are not dealt with.

One solution is *peer counseling*, which is based on the conviction that older persons can provide unique insight into the problems of other older persons because of their similar life experiences.

Project PACE was begun to test this particular approach. *PACE* is an acronym for *Psychological Alternative Counseling for Elders* and is a nonprofit agency that offers mental health services to older adults in Orange County, California. The PACE program was conceived and founded by Christopher Hayes, who worked six years as an orderly in nursing homes while working his way through college; his goal was to prepare himself for a career that would help keep older persons out of nursing homes. He was determined to find other alternatives to long-term institutional care.

The agency's two licensed counselors and a part-time social worker conduct weekly support groups at six county senior centers, and volunteer counselors visit most clients in their homes. This is important because many older persons in need of counseling are unable or unwilling to seek help; that help must be delivered to senior centers, nutrition sites, or individual homes. Each volunteer counselor has a caseload of five to seven persons.

The older adults are given a nine-week course in the fundamentals and techniques of counseling. There is no pretense that peer counselors can replace mental health professionals, but the volunteers can learn to recognize problems, offer crisis intervention, and refer clients to professionals when necessary. Basically, the peer counselor helps as a nonjudgmental listener and friend, who occasionally can draw upon his or her own experiences to help others cope with the difficulties of advancing age.

Hayes screens potential peer counselors, of course. He looks for flexibility and a willingness to learn new patterns of relating to other people. Many come from other volunteer programs, such as Meals on Wheels, where the volunteers have observed unmet emotional needs. The volunteers who are accepted into the program are highly motivated. Many are retired nurses, teachers, or businesspersons. "These are people who are not satisfied with the weekly golf or bridge game," Hayes affirms.

He acknowledges that a nine-week course is rudimentary. "However, over the course of their lives, older adults often have acquired the skills necessary to develop a warm and trusting relationship with another person," Hayes says. "What the PACE training does is to instruct the older volunteer in the most effective way to use these interpersonal skills, rather than to attempt to train the volunteer as a mental professional."

For further information about this program, write: PACE, P.O. Box 3372, Santa Ana, CA 92703.

You may also want to refer to the OASIS program described in Chapter 3.

Part Five

Meeting Basic Growth Needs

14

Education
You're Never Too Old to Learn

The saying "You're never too old to learn" has endured for generations because it is so true. My investigation proves that another version of this familiar adage is also true: "You're never too old to teach." Successful senior citizen programs affirm each adage, and many of us know elderly persons like Winona, our first landlady, who is now in her eighties.

Each Christmas Winona's card tells us about some new trip she has taken. In 1984 it was a cruise with her beloved Chicago Cubs. She has traveled around the world and seen the places she studied about in school. She lives on her pension and saves the money she makes from baby-sitting to pay for those annual trips.

Many older persons love to travel. As long as health and funds allow, travel with one exception is available to elderly persons everywhere. The exception is freighter travel: passengers above the age of seventy-five are not accepted.

We have seen how trips play a major role in senior centers and church-sponsored programs. Most of these are purely for fun, but traveling is a sure way of broadening and increasing knowledge.

A fascinating short-tour program called the *Road Runners* is directed by Father Declan Madden, O.F.M., of Denver. He described the program in the Summer 1982 issue of *Activities, Adaptation, and Aging* magazine. Or you can write him for information at 1060 St. Francis Way, Denver, CO 80204.

Elderhostel

This program is described as something for "elder citizens on the move"—not just in terms of travel, but in the sense of reaching out to new experiences. *Elderhostel*, inspired by youth hostels and the folk schools of Europe, is now a network of more than seven hundred colleges and universities in the United States and several other countries.

Most programs begin Sunday evening and end Saturday morning, although some of the overseas opportunities last for two or three weeks. Most classes are limited to thirty-five to forty-five participants who must be sixty years of age or older. Costs average $200 per week, which includes room and board but not transportation. College dormitories and facilities are utilized. It is a year-round program, no longer limited to summer or vacation weeks.

Courses include art, ecology, archaeology, music, language study, and much more. Here are a few samples from the 1985 catalog: Historical People of the Ozarks, New England Literature, Exploring Carl Jung, The Dilemma of Evil, Overcoming Computerphobia, and Techniques of Year-round Gardening (taught in California). You can study the Spanish language and Hispanic culture in Mexico, "Life at the Wall" in Berlin, or "The Holy Land of Three Major Faiths" in Israel. Remember, these are just samplings of several hundred courses available each *season* of the year.

A senior version of "Camp Farthest Out" is sponsored by an Illinois university through the Elderhostel program. It provides people over sixty with an opportunity to experience the physical and emotional risks of spending a week in the wilderness. They brave obstacle courses, learn to rappel, explore caves, and carry forty-pound backpacks to wilderness campsites. For information about this unusual educational program, write: Touch of Nature Environmental Center, Southern Illinois University, Carbondale, IL 62901.

What you can do. Share this information with active older members in your community. If you are over sixty, explore the opportunity for yourself. Get others to join with you.

Where to write: Elderhostel, 80 Boylston St., Suite 400, Boston, MA 02116.

Elderhostelers traveling overseas might want to contact "A Will/A Way," 59 Tahattawan Rd., Littleton, MA 01460.

Lifetime Learning Institute

This is a *local* program of continuing education, initiated by the American Association of Retired Persons.

In Austin, Texas, the program is carried out in cooperation with the Austin Community College. A recent fall program offered forty-four noncredit courses, held mostly in the daytime, two hours a week for eight weeks.

The Institute is a nonprofit program and is staffed by volunteers. Some instructors receive a small stipend. A $10 fee is charged for each course. The program is able to function economically because so many civic organizations and churches provide facilities for the classes at no charge.

A few of the courses offered in Austin are these: Porcelain Painting, Calligraphy, Conversational German, Making Money Last—Investments and Tax Planning, Microcomputers, Nutrition, and Genealogy. Classes are usually limited to fifteen persons, to insure a satisfactory teacher-student ratio.

What you can do. If an institute already exists in your community, volunteer your services as an instructor or staff person. Publicize the institute in your church or group. Encourage older members to sign up for specific classes.

Where to write: If no institute presently exists in your community, contact the Institute of Lifetime Learning, AARP, 1909 K St., NW, Washington, DC 20049. Request information on how to initiate a local program.

Lecture Series

Many senior centers offer lecture programs. An outstanding effort is the "Distinguished Lecture Series" sponsored by the

Senior Center of Palo Alto. A recent series was called "New Approaches to Social Policy Issues" and featured local professors and insiders involved with policy-making. As many as two hundred persons attended.

For information, write the Senior Center of Palo Alto, 450 Bryant St., Palo Alto, CA 94301.

Another fascinating venture was the "Senior Citizen Humanities Enrichment Project," sponsored by the Chicago Public Library. Its rationale was that many older persons were unable to complete their higher education because of the economic depression or other factors, but were still curious about their world. Thus, the humanities studies included literature, philosophy, history, and the arts. Exhibits from the Chicago Art Institute were often included, and the programs were led by local volunteer professors. Each course lasted eight weeks and was made available to the library system's seventy-seven branches, as well as to retirement residences, nursing homes, public housing projects, and senior clubs.

Unfortunately, this program became a casualty of federal funding cut-backs, but the idea might be tried elsewhere. For information, write the Coordinator, Services to Senior Citizens, Chicago Public Library, 425 N. Michigan Ave., Chicago, IL 60611.

Enrichment Education in Nursing Homes

There are several new approaches to education in long-term health facilities that merit attention. One might be called *outreach*—a delivered service to residents. The other is enrichment education for which residents themselves are largely responsible.

Education by Extension

Betsy Collins lives in Statesville, North Carolina, and is an artist by profession and training. Her older sister had a stroke several years ago, with resulting paralysis and aphasia. That stroke, along with facing the terminal illness of a very close friend, had a profound effect on "Aunt Betsy." In her grief, she decided to do something to help other people, especially older persons such as her sister.

What emerged was an idea that continuing education could be and should be taken into nursing homes. The University of North Carolina system offers a variety of continuing education programs to all of its citizens, and persons past sixty-five may participate in these programs without having to pay a fee. That gave Betsy her motivation.

CETA (the Comprehensive Employment and Training Act) employed her for the first year, followed by a staff arrangement with Mitchell Junior College, which was part of the state's continuing education system.

Aunt Betsy wasn't interested in becoming just another "activities director"; not that she had anything against a structured activities program. She was committed to providing enrichment courses in nursing homes, courses that would be more than socialization or busy-work, courses that would even provide college credit!

Since she had organized the local Arts Council, Aunt Betsy began with what she knew best. She began with a crafts class that used clay, not with molds, but using clay in what she calls "hand-building" projects. Collins makes it clear that her students are not handicapped, but merely limited in some way. The class is both instructive and therapeutic. As they work at their sculpture, they share jokes and stories. To secure credit, classes must meet six hours each week for eleven weeks. You can learn a lot about your subject and each other during that period of time.

During the nearly seven years that Collins has been working in this project, fourteen different courses have been developed. These have been offered in three different nursing homes. One was in a rural area. It had eighty residents, and sixty signed up for classes (although not all of these ultimately attended). Another was a retirement residence for economically deprived persons; it had no professional nursing staff but did include a half-way house for mentally retarded persons. The third was a large corporation-owned facility of 120 residents.

Aunt Betsy was helped by three paid staff persons and other

volunteers. She created or adapted much of her curriculum because she found very little that was written for elderly people "with limited physical and mental capabilities."

Here are brief descriptions of some of the things she developed.

There was a garden class, called "environmental science," that inspired twenty-two residents. There was discussion about earth and sea, but the hands-on gardening opportunity was its most popular aspect. Residents brought sickly plants from their rooms. They spaded a garden outdoors, with the help of four volunteer helpers. Several planter tables were built just high enough off the ground so that wheelchair-bound students could slide under them to work. Vegetables and flowers were grown, which were shared with others in the facility.

One course was called "cultural anthropology." Aunt Betsy points out that so many of these western North Carolinians were once poor dirt farmers, or were disadvantaged in other ways, and had little opportunity for education. She recognized their thirst for knowledge and felt that a discussion group would be the best way to proceed. Films are used to share a common experience, which can then be analyzed and discussed. Resources from the library are researched.

There was a current events class designed just for men. Aunt Betsy observes that male residents have less visitors than women, that the men appear to be very lonely and welcome the opportunity to talk. The men were urged to bring an article from a newspaper or magazine, and this would be discussed over a cup of coffee.

Another course was a math refresher. It is taught in a game format, played much like bingo but with the purpose of remembering multiplication tables and the principles of adding, subtracting, and simple division. It is a great way to keep minds alert.

There were Bible survey courses, with each resident bringing his or her Bible and notebook.

And Aunt Betsy has not forgotten her first love—art. She has had to make some adjustments, but she will not tolerate any "plastic cup decoration" that some people call "art." She asks the question, "If I were in this person's shoes, what would I miss the most?" She concentrates on working with things from nature—pressing flowers or making beautiful things from seashells. She encourages folk crafts, within the ability of the mountainfolk who were once expert in traditional early American craftsmanship. Aunt Betsy does concede to using more modern materials, however.

How to begin. Check with your state university system to see if a similar continuing education program might be delivered to nursing homes in your area. State or local funding from educational sources would be helpful, of course. More importantly, staff support may be available. Discuss the possibility of this kind of program in nursing homes with retired teachers or other interested persons. Get all of the help that you can! Find a suitable nursing home and secure the cooperation of an enthusiastic administrator. Experiment with a single course and evaluate. Begin simply and learn as you go.

Where to write: Betsy Collins, 128 Briarwood Rd., Statesville, NC 28677.

Music Education

The use of music has long been recognized as helpful therapy for confused persons. Stroke victims whose left hemisphere of the brain has been damaged will have difficulty with speech. However, if their right hemisphere was not affected, they will be able to respond to music and images. Another example is the stutterer. A person with this kind of speech impediment demonstrates it only in speech; it disappears when that person sings.

Most so-called musical therapy in nursing homes, unfortunately, borrows more from kindergartens than music education classes. There are rhythm bands and sing-alongs, but little of educational value. Moravian College of Bethlehem, Pennsylvania, is changing this approach. Dr. Paul Larson, professor of music education at Moravian College, now includes teaching music to elderly persons as well as to the young in his music education courses.

Two nursing homes were chosen that already had some kind

of music program. The idea was to go beyond activity and therapy, toward significant new musical learning.

In one home, a student teacher worked with a chorus. She gave voice lessons to a woman who had always wanted to sing. She taught piano to another resident who had "forgotten all she ever knew about playing the piano." A concert was given at the end of the semester. Many of the performers were in wheelchairs, but sang and even moved about in a stylized choreography to recorded classical music. The woman who wanted to learn to sing, sang a solo—accompanied by the lady who had forgotten how to play the piano.

In the second home, a team of student teachers taught residents how to play recorders, autoharps, bells, and percussion instruments. Filmstrips about composers and their music were shown and discussed. Residents learned to sing and play music from all five continents.

One of the more spectacular students was Lou. She was a ninety-three-year-old retired school teacher who loved music and would still attempt to sing and dance. She was obviously talented but did not know how to play any musical instrument. She began with the bells and graduated to the autoharp. In time, she could play all of the songs without any prompting or cues. The teachers recognized true musical achievement.

This is an example of education for older persons that goes beyond novelty and busy-work to meaningful learning.

Others can do it, too, especially music teachers and church choir directors. Handbells could be shared, as well as band and orchestra instruments for those who once played them.

For information about the Moravian College program, write: Moravian College, Music Dept., Bethlehem, PA 18018.

Another quick example: the *Eskaton Sunrise Chorus*. Its director is only twenty-two years old, but the average age of the choristers is eighty-one (the oldest member is ninety-six). Three of the members sing from their wheelchairs. The chorus began as a Christmas project and now performs at retirement and nursing homes throughout the Sacramento, California, area. *Eskaton* itself is a retirement community.

Close Harmony is a beautiful film about an intergenerational music program between fourth and fifth graders and a senior citizens' chorus. It won the 1982 Academy Award for Best Documentary Short Film. For information, contact: Learning Corporation of America, 1350 Avenue of the Americas, New York, NY 10019.

Senior Citizens Teaching Others

A third approach to continuing education in nursing homes is by way of residents initiating an educational project themselves. Practically, of course, they will need help and support—and sometimes advice—from outside their circle.

Residents in a nursing home in Silver Spring, Maryland, were unusually alert and concerned about their opportunities to be helpful to each other and to others. They held a bake sale to secure money to help a well-loved aide continue her education in professional health care. They "adopted" residents in another nursing home on the other side of the city, whom they visited as they were able. But they wanted to do more.

A day care center for children was located just across the street. The children visited the nursing home from time to time, and the residents loved the intergenerational interaction, which is an extravagant way of saying they simply came to love these children.

They learned that the children lacked a playhouse. So the residents decided they would provide one. What they really decided was that they would *make* one!

They held another bake sale to raise money for materials. Their activity coordinator found a volunteer to help them—an instructor in shop and carpentry at the local high school. He spent three to four hours each week, helping the residents decide on plans, and then helped them transform those plans into reality.

The residents chose to build a playhouse with a Scandinavian design. It was probably the most complicated design they could have chosen, because it included a front porch with some fancy railings. The project took almost a year to complete. The volunteer instructor expected that the men would be more interested and adept, but was happily surprised to discover how the ladies wanted to help. Many of them learned to use carpentry tools for the first time in their lives.

Finally, the playhouse was completed—painted inside and out, roof shingled, and weatherized for outdoor use. The playhouse was covered with a huge sheet, as though it were a statue, and the children were invited to a party for the unveiling. A local television station videotaped the event for the community to enjoy.

The learning in this experiment occurred in planning, teamwork, and manual arts. Few people would have dreamed that residents of a nursing home could tackle a project that was so physically demanding. They did, they succeeded, and their reward was the great outpouring of joy from the children.

Another area of education in nursing homes is for residents to be recruited as resource-teachers in the local school system.

A high school social studies class in Maryland decided to explore "home remedies and superstitions." They set up a time to meet with interested residents at a nearby nursing home. The teacher and the students explained their project and said they thought many of the residents could help them by recalling things they had learned in their youth. It was decided that the class would visit the nursing home every other week and that a team of residents would visit the high school during alternate weeks. The result: an exciting exchange of facts and folklore.

There were at least two ongoing spin-off results from this experience.

First, the contact with students in their classes continued. Here were real live persons who could describe how to make butter in a butter churn or what life was like during World War I. Students and residents took occasional visits to the local museum, and the nursing home residents were able to add interesting facts and insights to what was being observed. There were even a few times when the elderly members of this group would talk about the reality of wheelchair life, incontinency, or death—as they now saw and experienced it.

A similar experiment took place in DeFuniak Springs, Florida. Residents there were called "elderly teachers" who taught "living history."

The residents benefited by being needed and useful, as well as by remembering facts and circumstances they had long forgotten. The high school students learned more than facts and experiences: they discovered that older people, even nursing home residents, are people with personal histories and private dignity.

For more information about these programs in nursing homes, write:

Joan Betzold, Manor Healthcare Corporation, 10720 Columbia Pike, Silver Spring, MD 20901.

Dennis Goodman, Beverly Enterprises, 3284 Virginia Beach Blvd., No. 200, Virginia Beach, VA 23452.

There are other refreshing examples of older persons teaching others. Older persons in California and Michigan tutor migrant workers and their children. In Tacoma, Washington, the tutors are organized as *RAISE* (Retirees Active In Student Education). Oldsters throughout the nation assist in G.E.D. (General Education Development) and English-as-a-second-language classes, and tax forums. Members of SCORE (Service Corps of Retired Executives) help novice businessmen through the Small Business Administration.

This is the road to self-actualization, meeting the needs for human growth: self-fulfillment, achievement, and meaningfulness. There are basic needs to meet first. But since people do not live by bread alone, we can be inspired by the example of older people who feed the mind.

We're never too old to learn, or to teach.

Part Six

Meeting Miscellaneous Needs

15

Potpourri
Ideas for Innovators

At this stage I find that I have a file of leftover odds-and-ends of programs and projects, as well as a few ideas of my own of the "Why doesn't somebody try this?" variety. None of these seem to fit conveniently into the preceding chapters, so I will suggest them here, with a hope that something may trigger your positive response and further investigation.

A Directory of Barrier-free Facilities

Access Austin is an eighty-two-page booklet, a "Guide to Austin for Mobility-Impaired Persons." It contains information on more than two hundred buildings and facilities (which includes restaurants, theatres, churches, museums, libraries, etc.) in terms of parking areas, curb cuts and ramps, interiors, and rest rooms. The booklet includes information of special interest to blind and deaf persons. It was published as a volunteer project of *MIGHT* (Mobility Impaired Grappling Hurdles Together). In years past, we found the guide to be extremely helpful as we looked for interesting, barrier-free places to take Carolyn's dad.

Making such a guide would be a good service project for a group in your community.

For more information, write: MIGHT, Austin Resource Center for Independent Living, 2818 San Gabriel St., Austin, TX 78705.

Special Shopping for Seniors

Many businesses offer special discounts to senior citizens, which help older persons stretch their dollars. TARGET department stores go an extra mile. Early in December, TARGET stores schedule a "senior citizens and handicapped shopping event." For two hours, from 9 A.M. to 11 A.M., its stores are closed to the general public. Buses are rented and ambulatory residents of nursing homes, along with other older persons, are delivered to the stores, treated to free coffee and doughnuts, and given the freedom of an uncrowded store to browse and shop. Store personnel are there to help and to provide free gift-wrapping. It probably doesn't create a lot of cash revenue for TARGET, but they reap a lot of good will.

Since TARGET stores are not located everywhere, the idea could be tried by other firms.

For information about the TARGET program, write: Dayton-Hudson Corporation, 777 Nicollet Mall, Minneapolis, MN 55402.

Free Telephone Calls

A major stock brokerage firm makes its long distance WATS lines available at Christmastime to older persons. They sign up, in advance, at the local Adult Services Council, and volunteers pick them up on Saturday morning at their residences or nursing homes. They sit at desks normally occupied by Merrill Lynch Pierce Fenner & Smith stockbrokers and are told they can call anyone, anywhere, for as long as they like. The program was begun in 1983.

Fifteen people were given the telephone treat in Austin last Christmas; and while one person called friends in London, England, and Madrid, Spain, most calls were regional. One man called his brother in Odessa, located in west Texas. "This was the first time I've ever telephoned him in my life," he said. "I haven't seen him to speak to him since 1972."

The brokerage firm employees helped place the calls and

brought coffee, hot chocolate, cider, and cookies, along with providing the Christmas "bells."

More on Telephones

We have already discussed telephone reassurance programs, which are simply one person calling another at some agreed-upon schedule.

New York City has a program called *Telephone Family*. It is a conference call, set up regularly through the telephone company, in which selected isolated adults have an opportunity to talk with an expert about Medicare, consumer rights, tax questions, and so on. For information, write: Jewish Association for Services to the Aged, 40 W. 68th St., New York, NY 10023.

A somewhat similar but larger program is the *Phone-A-Friend* party-line service offered by NYNEX, the telephone company that now serves the Northeast.

Phone-A-Friend links five people on a party line, so they can chat or just listen. As many as 120 callers in twenty-four clusters can use the network simultaneously. When someone drops out by hanging up, the line is open for someone else to join. The telephone company provides moderators who monitor the calls, disconnect unwanted callers, and help keep the conversation going. Charges to callers range from 11 to 24 cents for the first minute and 3 to 8 cents for each subsequent minute, depending on where the caller lives.

This experimental program, begun in the spring of 1984, is limited to 170,000 residential customers in thirty-seven exchanges on Long Island and Staten Island, New York.

Helping the Elderly Poor Stay Warm

The Metropolitan Inter-Faith Association of Memphis has made an arrangement with the Memphis Light, Gas, and Water Division whereby its customers voluntarily agree to have one dollar added to each month's utility bill. This "Plus 1" program provides funds for emergency services and a weatherization program administered by the ecumenical organization.

For more information, write: MIFA, P.O. Box 3130, Memphis, TN 38173-0208.

Special Radio and TV Programming

Many broadcasters make a good living not from *broad*casting but from *narrow*casting—programming to youth, to racial-ethnics, to Christians, to lovers of classical music, and to other substantial but not necessarily mass segments of the available audience. Two Massachusetts educational radio stations schedule programming for older adults.

WMFO-FM, operated by Tufts University, offers a daily interview program called "Across the Ages." Its address is WMFO-FM, Tufts University, P.O. Box 65, Medford, MA 02155.

WUMB-FM, operated by the University of Massachusetts, has a two-hour Monday-through-Friday program called "As Young As You Feel." It features music from the thirties through the fifties, as well as an issue-oriented "Elder Review" segment. Its address is WUMB-FM, University of Massachusetts/Boston, Harbor Campus, Boston, MA 02125.

KRDO-TV, Channel 13 in Colorado Springs, Colorado, employs a retired newscaster to report on news and activities of special interest to older viewers. It is a regular feature on the evening news. The station's address is KRDO-TV, 399 S. 8th St., Colorado Springs, CO 80905.

Bookmobiles

Since OPEC raised our fuel prices, bookmobiles have been disappearing from public library programs. The older, huge gas-guzzlers probably cannot be justified today from a cost-effectiveness point of view. However, a smaller van, equipped with large-print books, a few best-sellers, and records could perform a valuable service to the homebound and the roombound in nursing homes.

Discuss the idea with your library commission, library administration, or city council. And if delivered library services cannot be initiated (or resumed), an individual with his or her automobile can still take significant reading and listening matter to wherever the older taxpayers live.

Drama

"Acting Up!" is a senior adult performing troupe sponsored by Oakton Community College in Des Plaines, Illinois. It is an improvisational drama group, organized in 1978. Each member is over the age of sixty.

The troupe's purpose is to dispel the myths and stereotypes of aging, which it does through a series of vignettes and a slide presentation. The group performs forty to fifty times a year in schools, senior centers, churches and synagogues, and to civic groups. The members meet once a week to rehearse and write new material, most of this growing out of their own life experiences. A community library donates rehearsal space and use of its auditorium. Funding comes from the community college and the Skokie Fine Arts Commission.

The troupe often performs at workshops where issues facing older persons are studied.

For more information, write: Office of Community Services, Oakton Community College, 1600 East Golf Rd., Des Plaines, IL 60016.

As they grow older, persons who have been active in Little Theatre groups find little to challenge them as actors. Roles are stereotyped or nonexistent in many popular plays. A group was formed to meet this challenge, called the *American Theatre Association Senior Adult Theatre*.

It solicits new scripts from playwrights, as well as appropriate material from publishers of plays. A "Most Promising New Play for Senior Adult Theatre" award is made annually.

Plays are chosen that will challenge elderly actors, no matter what their level of experience or competence might be. Selections are judged on how they depict growing older, whether this is done with unusual insight and charm, with wit, and with patience. The plays feature older persons in positive roles that lift up the values of growing older.

An annual play list is published, for which there is a charge. The 1983 listing describes twenty-five plays.

For information write: Bonnie L. Vorenberg, 6816 N. Villard Ave., Portland, OR 97217.

Day Care for Children in a Nursing Home

A separate room was found in a Seattle nursing home, which was painted and equipped for a cheerful children's day care center. Called the "Hands Across the Years" project, selected residents from the nursing home were recruited as part-time helpers and surrogate grandparents. The children and the older adults sing and share together. The children learn about aging, nurturing, and death in ways that would never be possible in a conventional child-care environment. Twenty children are enrolled in the project.

Oral History Projects

In 1986 Texas will celebrate its 150th birthday, and the Sesquicentennial Commission is asking for help in developing special display and printed materials.

The Senior Programs division of Austin's Parks and Recreation Department has recruited a group of volunteers to visit older adults. They go with tape cassette recorders, looking for stories and reminiscences from the elderly about the good and not-so-good old days. They are also seeking old photographs, which will be copied and returned, to be used in special commemorative displays.

This is a good project for any city or county library that houses, or could house, a historical collection about its area and region. It is a good project for families, too—to capture memories and images while these are still available.

A good way to begin is to read *Good Times with Old Times* by

Katie Funk Wiebe, published by Herald Press. It is a guide on how to write memoirs.

The Postman Rings at Least Once

In rural areas of Sweden, the postman maintains a special relationship with older persons. He is both mobile post office and bank. In addition, he does shopping and even carries special containers for milk and butter. He gives advice on welfare rights and takes messages to and from social services. Postal employees meet once a month with Swedish social services people to learn about new developments.

We may not soon see this kind of outreach accepted by the U.S. Postal Service. However, mail carriers do play an important role in being aware of elderly patrons and their welfare. Mail carriers and meter readers are often the best sources for reporting emergencies, illness, or abuse that affects the elderly.

Investment of Life

Lillian Carter, President Jimmy Carter's mother, became a Peace Corps worker in India in her retirement years. The Presbyterian Church (USA) has a short-term program called "Volunteers In Mission," which is a kind of VISTA or Peace Corps program, both in the United States and overseas. Qualified retirees offer their skills and experience for housing and transportation; they receive no pay.

Two of my good friends, both in their seventies, have just completed a three-month work project with Koinonia and the Habitat housing project in Americus, Georgia.

Carolyn keeps asking me why more churches don't have a deaconess program, similar to what is available in Europe. I don't have the answer. Of course, most denominations now elect both men and women as church officers, but this isn't quite the same thing as the *deaconess* who is an employed church worker to visit the sick and homeless within a parish. Perhaps we need to revive an ancient church office. It would be an ideal vocation for many retired women—and men.

Postscripts

I'm often asked, "Where do you get all of these ideas?" I get them from newspaper items and books, from an occasional feature on TV, from articles in *AGING* magazine (published by the Department of Human Services), and from meeting new friends in workshops and on media talk-shows.

This is not a complete list of what people can do in compassionate care for the aging. It is a beginning and I hope you will find a way to continue and discover some particular ministry which needs a sponsor and a sparkplug wherever it is that you live.

You can look for new ideas and approaches too. Scan your newspaper. Listen and watch for innovative, helpful projects. Brainstorm with your group; without reinventing wheels—programs that already exist—develop your own special ways of meeting a specific need of older people.

I would like to hear from you because your experiences and ideas might find their way into a second edition of this book. My address is 9303 Hunters Trace East, Austin, TX 78758.

May your search and research be happy and helpful to our older friends.

Appendix A

SENIOR ADULT NEEDS and INTERESTS SURVEY

Survey of Older Adults in the Community
(duplicate on 5 x 7 cards, or sheet of paper)

General Information

NAME _____

1. Age Last Birthday   ADDRESS _____
   0 ____ 60-64
   0 ____ 65-74
   0 ____ 75 and over   BIRTH DATE _____

2. Marital Status   TELEPHONE _____
   0 ____ Spouse Living   REMARKS: _____
   0 ____ Widowed
   0 ____ Never Married

3. Church Participation
   0 ____ Morning Worship _____
   0 ____ Evening Worship _____
   0 ____ Sunday School _____
   0 ____ Church Training _____
   0 ____ Mission
          Organizations
   0 ____ Prayer Meeting   Interviewed by _____
                            Date _____

4. Spiritual Enrichment   0
5. Weekday Bible Study   0
6. Discussion and
   Prayer Group   0
7. Book Studies   0
8. Retreats   0
9. Other
   Name _____   0

10. Learning Opportunities   0
11. Religions   0
12. Personal Enrichment   0
13. Arts and Crafts   0
14. Hobbies   0
15. Manual Skills   0
16. Current Events   0
17. Other
    Name _____   0 •

From *How to Minister to Senior Adults in Your Church* by Horace Kerr. Copyright © 1980 by Broadman Press. All rights reserved. Used by permission.

0	**18. Socialization**
0 _____	19. Fellowship with Peers
0 _____	20. Fellowship with Other Ages
0 _____	21. Arts and Crafts Name _____
0 _____	22. Hobby Groups Name _____
0 _____	23. Music Activities
0 _____	24. Drama
0 _____	25. Table Games
0 _____	26. Sports Participation Name _____
0 _____	27. Trips
0 _____	28. Retreats
0 _____	29. Church Club

30. Service Opportunities	0
31. General Office Work	_____ 0
32. Library Work	_____ 0
33. Lawn Work	_____ 0
34. Home Repairs	_____ 0
35. Transportation	_____ 0
36. Visit	_____ 0
37. Telephone	_____ 0
38. Teach Arts, Crafts, Hobbies	_____ 0
39. Witness	_____ 0
40. Music	_____ 0
41. Mission Work	_____ 0
42. Work with Youth	_____ 0
43. Work with Children	_____ 0
44. Community Programs	_____ 0

---

45. SERVICES NEEDED

0 _____	46. Transportation
0 _____	47. Health
0 _____	48. Finances
0 _____	49. Employment
0 _____	50. Nutrition
0 _____	51. Housing

53. Home Repairs	_____ 0
54. Homemaker	_____ 0
55. Friendly Visits	_____ 0
56. Telephone Reassurance	_____ 0
57. Shopping Assistance	_____ 0
58. Daycare	_____ 0

0 _____ 52. Other: _____

Date of this survey _____

SURVEY OF OLDER ADULT PROGRAMS IN THE CHURCH

Church _____

Program _____

Time frame of program:

Monthly? _____ (Month _____ to month _____)

Year-round? _____ Weekly? _____ (What day? _____)

Description of program: _____

_____

_____

How is this supportive of older adults? _____

_____

How many participants? _____

How many are older adults? _____

Accountable to which church committee? _____

_____

What is the cost to participants? _____

To the congregation?_____

What congregational facilities are used? _____

_____

How long has this program been in existence?_____

What are future plans?_____

_____

SURVEY OF COMMUNITY AGENCIES

Name of agency _____

Contact person _____ Telephone _____

Address _____

Purpose _____

What services are available to older adults?_____

_____

_____

What can volunteers do? _____

_____

What charges are made to participants? _____

_____

What can this congregation do to help your agency? _____

_____

Date of this survey _____ (Review/update annually)

Note: attach an annual report or descriptive brochure.

Appendix B

Ten Typical Menus of Meals Served in a Senior Center

1. Ham and Scalloped
   Potatoes
   Grated Carrot and Raisin
   Salad
   Chocolate Pudding

2. Fish Squares
   Macaroni and Cheese
   Spinach
   Sliced Tomatoes
   Strawberry Jello

3. Beef-A-Roni
   Whole Kernel Corn
   Apple Sauce
   Ice Cream with Chocolate
   Sauce

4. Meat Loaf
   Browned Potatoes
   Sliced Carrots
   Tossed Vegetable Salad
   Raisin Cake with Sauce

5. Baked Fish
   Cheese-Rice
   Stewed Tomatoes
   Lettuce Wedge
   Apricots

6. Grilled Franks with Cheese
   Baked Beans
   Tossed Green Salad
   Bread Pudding

7. Liver and Onions
   Rice
   Buttered Carrots with
   Pimento
   Sliced Cucumbers
   Ice Cream with Cherry Sauce

8. Spaghetti and Meat Sauce
   Spinach
   Cole Slaw
   Canned Fruit

9. Fresh Perch Fillet
   Parsley Noodles
   Collard Greens
   Sliced Tomatoes
   Plums

10. Hamburgers
    French Fried Potatoes
    Harvard Beets
    Grated Apple and Celery
    Salad
    Rice Pudding

Five Large-Quantity Recipes

Potato Soup (serves 25)

(Courtesy of the Dietetic Dept., Saint David's Community Hospital, Austin, Texas.)

9 quarts of hot milk
3/4 pound (1 1/2 cups) butter or margarine, melted
1 1/2 cups flour
3 tablespoons salt
1/2 teaspoon pepper, white
12 pounds potatoes, peeled and diced
1 cup onion, chopped
1 cup celery, chopped

Boil the potatoes, onions, and celery in three quarts of water until soft. Drain.

Melt the butter in a pot large enough to hold 2 1/2 gallons and remove from heat. Add the flour, stirring until smooth. Add the salt and pepper. Gradually add the hot milk, stirring constantly. Over medium heat, cook and stir as necessary until the cream sauce is smooth and thick. To this cream sauce add the potatoes, onions, and celery. The potatoes may be mashed or pureed, if a smoother soup is desired.

From Carolyn's kitchen...

Texas Hash (serves 25)

6 onions, chopped
6 green peppers, chopped
6 cups celery, chopped
6 pounds ground lean meat
1/2 pound margarine
3 teaspoons chili powder
6 teaspoons salt
1 teaspoon pepper
3 cups rice
3 cans (No. 2 1/2) peeled tomatoes

Brown meat with vegetables; add seasoning. Place in large baking dish or pan. Sprinkle uncooked rice on top. Do not stir. Add tomatoes. Cover dish and bake at 350 degrees for 2 hours. Sprinkle broken tacos with grated cheese on top.

Brunswick Stew (serves 24)

24 chicken parts
3/4 cup bacon drippings
3 quarts water
2 cups chopped onion
6 cans (No. 2 1/2) tomatoes
2 bay leaves
1 tablespoon Worcestershire sauce
4 10-oz. pkgs. frozen okra
4 10-oz. pkgs. frozen lima beans
4 10-oz. pkgs. frozen corn
1 tablespoon salt

Dust chicken in flour and brown in heavy skillet. Place in large stew pot. Cover with water. Add onion, tomatoes, and seasoning. Simmer 2 hours. Just before serving, add vegetables and cook 10 minutes. Serve with mashed potatoes, cooked rice, or homemade bread.

Beef Stroganoff (serves 24)

2 quarts sour cream
1 cup shortening
8 pounds thinly sliced beef
3 3/4 quarts water
1 six oz. can tomato paste
1 quart chopped onions
3 pounds mushrooms, sliced
2/3 cup flour
1 1/8 cup beef consommé
1 tablespoon salt
1 tablespoon paprika

Brown meat, add water and tomato paste, simmer for 2 hours. Sauté onions and mushrooms; add consommé. Make paste of flour and add to broth. Stir in sour cream just before serving. Serve hot over rice or noodles.

Chicken Marengo (serves 24)

10 chickens, halved and seasoned
1 quart salad oil
1/8 pound butter or margarine
1/2 clove garlic
1/2 gallon chicken stock
1/4 gallon tomato sauce
1/4 gallon brown gravy
2 pounds mushrooms

Sauté chickens, place in roasting pans. Mix other ingredients, simmer 20 minutes, add to chickens. Bake 45 minutes, 350 degrees. Serve with rice or noodles.

Appendix C

Federal Funding Sources for Adult Day Care Services

Reference is made in the following listing to several federal agencies. To locate your nearest office, consult the blue pages of your telephone directory or request information from the following:

Department of Health and Human Services
200 Independence Ave., SW
Washington, DC 20201

Department of Labor
200 Constitution Ave., NW
Washington, DC 20210

Department of Education
400 Maryland Ave., SW
Washington, DC 20202

Department of Transportation
400 Seventh St., SW
Washington, DC 20590

Department of the Treasury
1500 Pennsylvania Ave., NW
Washington, DC 20220

Department of Housing and Urban Development
451 Seventh St., SW
Washington, DC 20410
(also refer to regional listing in Appendix D)

ACTION
806 Connecticut Ave., NW
Washington, DC 20525

ADMINISTRATIVE AGENCY STATUTE TITLE AND SECTION PROGRAM NAME

1. *HEALTH CARE FINANCING ADMINISTRATION, DHHS*

- *Social Security Act of 1974, PL 93-647*

  Title XIX, Grants to States for medical assistance programs

  Medicaid

Adult Day Care Services Uses And Restrictions

Medical day care for Medicaid eligibles, reimbursed as clinic services or out-patient hospital services, can combine needed services included in the state plan as a day health care service package. Per diem rate is established by the state Medicaid agency. Some individual health services in a day care program not so reimbursed can be reimbursed as individual Medicaid services.

Applicant Procedure

Contact should be made with the state agency administering the Title XIX state plan.

2. *OFFICE OF HUMAN DEVELOPMENT SERVICES, ADMINISTRATION FOR PUBLIC SERVICES, DHHS*

- *Social Security Act of 1974, PL 93-647*

  Title XX, Section 2002 (a) (1)

  Social Services

Title XX funding of a day care program is primarily directed toward the social service components of such a program, including: social work evaluation and counseling; recreational activities, including those with a therapeutic goal such as reality orientation; nutritional services, including food and its preparation and serving; transportation and educational and training activities. Each state develops its own definition of day care in the Annual Comprehensive Services Program plan. It is possible to use Title XX funds to support the health components in a day care program but only under certain specified conditions.

Contact should be made with the state or local agency (Department of Social Services or Public Welfare) administering Title XX.

3. *OFFICE OF HUMAN DEVELOPMENT SERVICES, ADMINIS-TRATION ON AGING, DHHS*

• *Older Americans Act of 1965, PL 89-73*

Title III

Area Planning and Social Service Programs

Title III funds may be used to support transportation, social, recreational, and educational services which are not otherwise provided.

Contact should be made locally with the area Agency on Aging or at the state level with the state Agency on Aging.

4. *OFFICE OF HUMAN DEVELOPMENT SERVICES, ADMINIS-TRATION ON AGING, DHHS*

• *Older Americans Act of 1965, PL 89-73*

Title III, Section 308

Model Projects on Aging

These funds are awarded on a time-limited basis to support innovative programs, evaluation of which will contribute to national knowledge.

Funding decisions are made by the Administration on Aging central office with consideration given to recommendations made by state and area Agencies on Aging and regional Aging offices.

5. *OFFICE OF HUMAN DEVELOPMENT SERVICES, ADMINIS-TRATION ON AGING, DHHS*

• *Older Americans Act of 1965, PL 89-73*

Title VII

Nutrition

A day care center can be a Title VII site, providing a hot meal at least 5 days a week to participants over age 60. Title VII funds can also provide for nutrition education, recreational activities, and some other services, although support for the latter is usually sought elsewhere to conserve Title VII money for meals.

Contact should be made locally with the area Agency on Aging or at the state level with the state Agency on Aging.

6. *EMPLOYMENT AND TRAINING ADMINISTRATION, DEPART-MENT OF LABOR*

• *Older Americans Act of 1965, PL 89-73*

Title IX, Section 902 (b)

Senior Community Service Employment

As a subsidized employment program, Title IX can provide part-time staff for day care services. However, the goal of Title IX is to move these individuals into unsubsidized employment. Title IX employees must be economically disadvantaged and age 55+. Funds may also be used to provide training for Title IX staff and employees' transportation costs when performing their job.

Application should be made to national contractors and/or the state agency designated by the governor to administer these funds.

7. *ALCOHOL, DRUG ABUSE, AND MENTAL HEALTH ADMINIS-TRATION, PUBLIC HEALTH SERVICE, DHHS*

• *Mental Retardation Facilities and Community Mental Health Centers Construction Act of 1963, PL 94-63*

Titles I and III

Community mental health centers must provide partial hospital services, including but not limited to day care, day treatment, evening and weekend services, funded as part of a total package of community mental health services.

Contact the state Mental Health Authority or the Alcohol, Drug Abuse, and Mental Health Administration regional office.

8. *PUBLIC HEALTH SERVICE, HEALTH SERVICES ADMINIS-TRATION, DHHS*

• *Health Revenue Sharing Act of the Public Health Services Act of 1965, PL 94-63*

Title I, Section 102

Comprehensive Public Health Services

Can be used to fund day care services as determined by state health and mental health authorities. May be used to insure the availability of appropriate noninstitutional services for persons with mental health problems.

Contact should be made with state health and mental health administrative agencies.

9. *PUBLIC HEALTH SERVICE, HEALTH SERVICES ADMINISTRATION, DHHS*

- *Health Revenue Sharing Act of the Public Health Services Act of 1975, PL 94-63*

  Title V, Section 330

  Community Health Centers

Can be used to fund day care services as provided by community health centers or through contracts or cooperative arrangements with other public or private entities as arranged for by the community health center.

Contact should be made with locally designated community health centers.

10. *DEPARTMENT OF EDUCATION*

- *Adult Education Act, PL 91-230*
- *Community Education Act*
- *Higher Education Act of 1965, Title I*
- *Lifelong Learning, Part B, Education Amendments of 1976*
- *Vocational Education Act of 1963, as amended (Title II, Education Amendments of 1976)*
- *Women's Educational Equity Act*
- *Guidance and Counseling, Part D, Education Amendments of 1976*

Each of these programs may be looked to for funding of day care service components.

Contact should be made with the Department of Education regarding particular funding needs.

11. *ACTION*

- *Domestic Volunteer Service Act of 1973, PL 93-113*

  RSVP
  VISTA

RSVP and VISTA can provide volunteer personnel for day care services. RSVP can also provide transportation for the volunteers as needed. VISTA workers may receive placements not exceeding 2 years but not less than 1 year.

Contact state ACTION office.

12. *COMMUNITY SERVICES ADMINISTRATION*

- *Community Services Act of 1974, PL 93-644*

  Title II, Section 221 (a)

  Community Action Programs

Can be used to establish new or to fund existing day care programs for low-income elderly (as defined by CSA poverty guidelines) in urban and rural areas. In addition to funds available from Community Action agencies, the Community Services Administration may extend funding to public or nonprofit agencies capable of carrying out a day care program.

Contact state Economic Opportunity Office to locate appropriate local Community Action Agency.

13. *URBAN MASS TRANSIT ADMINISTRATION, DEPARTMENT OF TRANSPORTATION*

- *Urban Mass Transportation Act of 1964, PL 88-365, 93-503*

  Research and Demonstration Program

Funds may be provided to pay up to 80 percent of the cost of vehicles to a private nonprofit agency or a public agency when vehicles are covered by a local transportation plan. UMTA recommends that transportation be provided as part of a system, rather than assigning one vehicle to one program, in order to maximize the amount of transportation service provided.

Contact should be made with the Urban Mass Transit Administration.

14. *DEPARTMENT OF HOUSING AND URBAN DEVELOPMENT*

- *Housing and Community Development Act of 1974, PL 93-383*

  Title I, Section 5301-5317

  Community Development Block Grants

Can be used for developing, improving, and coordinating day care services to benefit low and inadequate income individuals. Money can be used as matching funds for other federal service programs. Program focuses on urban areas where there is a great need for physical redevelopment. While some money is available for services, priority in most communities is for neighborhood redevelopment, housing rehabilitation, etc.

Applications can be made to HUD regional field offices.

15. *UNITED STATES DEPARTMENT OF THE TREASURY*

• *State and Local Fiscal Assistance Act, PL 94-488*

Amendments 1976

General Revenue Sharing

Funds may be for program operations, staffing, and capital expenses. Revenue sharing funds may be used as a match for other federal funds. Since particular consideration is given to nonrecurring expenditures, these funds are applicable to the development of day care programs. A public hearing is required; senior citizens and their organizations should have the opportunity to be heard.

Procedure is highly localized. Contact local government (state, county, town, etc.). Provide input into plans for use of these funds (hearings, contact with agency heads). Examine plan in effect and state report of fund allocations. Approach key political and budgetary officials for guidance.

Appendix D

Agency Addresses

U.S. Department of Housing and Urban Development

Regional Offices
(Contact regional offices for your nearest field office address.)

Boston Regional Office
Room 800
John F. Kennedy Federal Building
Boston, MA 02203-0801

New York Regional Office
26 Federal Plaza
New York, NY 10278-0068

Philadelphia Regional Office
Curtis Building
6th and Walnut St.
Philadelphia, PA 19106-3392

Atlanta Regional Office
Richard B. Russell Federal Building
75 Spring St., SW
Atlanta, GA 30303-3388

Chicago Regional Office
300 S. Wacker Dr.
Chicago, IL 60606-6765

Fort Worth Regional Office
221 W. Lancaster
Fort Worth, TX 76113-2905

Kansas City Regional Office
Professional Building
1103 Grand Ave.
Kansas City, MO 64106-2496

Denver Regional Office
Executive Tower Building
1405 Curtis St.
Denver, CO 80202-2349

San Francisco Regional Office
Phillip Burton Federal Building
450 Golden Gate Ave.
San Francisco, CA 94102-3448

Seattle Regional Office
Arcade Plaza Building
1321 2nd Ave.
Seattle, WA 98101-2054

The Administration on Aging

Regional Offices

Region I (CI, ME, MA, NH, RI, VT)
John F. Kennedy Federal Bldg.
Government Center, Room 2007
Boston, MA 02203

Region II (NJ, NY, Puerto Rico, Virgin Islands)
26 Federal Plaza, Room 4106
New York, NY 10007

Region III (DE, MD, PA, VA, WV)
P.O. Box 13716
3535 Market St., 5th Floor
Philadelphia, PA 19101

Region IV (AL, FL, GA, KY, MS, NC, SC, TN)
101 Marietta Tower, 8th Floor
Atlanta, GA 30303

Region V (IL, IN, MI, MN, OH, WI)
300 S. Wacker Dr., 15th Floor
Chicago, IL 60606

Region VI (AR, LA, NM, OK, TX)
Fidelity Union Tower Bldg., Room 500
1507 Pacific Ave.
Dallas, TX 75201

Region VII (IA, KS, MO, NE)
601 E. 12th St.
Kansas City, MO 64106

Region VIII (CO, MT, ND, SD, UT, WY)
Federal Office Building, 7th Floor
19th and Stout St.
Denver, CO 80202

Region IX (AZ, CA, HI, NV, Samoa, Guam, Trust Territory)
50 U.N. Plaza, Room 206
San Francisco, CA 94102

Region X (AK, ID, OR, WA)
Arcade Plaza Bldg.
1321 2nd Ave.
Seattle, WA 98101

Shepherd's Centers Listing

Alabama

Eastern Area Shepherd's Center
118 N. 84th St.
Birmingham, AL 35206

Riley Community Center
3617 Hickory Ave. SW
Birmingham, AL 35221

United Methodist Center for Senior Citizens
4616 Terrace "R"
Birmingham, AL 35208

Arkansas

Shepherd's Center of Little Rock
600 Pleasant Valley Dr.
Little Rock, AR 72207

California

College Ave. Adult Center
College Ave. Baptist Church
4747 College Ave.
San Diego, CA 92115

Peninsula Shepherd's Center
1475 Catalina Blvd.
San Diego, CA 92107

Connecticut

Center Cities Churches/Services
136 Capitol Ave.
Hartford, CT 06106

Florida

The Life Center
819 Park St.
Jacksonville, FL 32204

Pinellas County Interfaith Coalition on Aging
11438 Oval Dr.
Largo, FL 33544

Life Enrichment Center
9704 North Blvd.
Tampa, FL 33612

Shepherd's Center of Hillsborough County
6111 Central Ave.
Tampa, FL 33604

Shepherd's Center
Saint Catherine's Episcopal Church
502 Druid Hills Rd.
Temple Terrace, FL 33617

Georgia

Life Enrichment Services
3715 La Vista Rd.
Decatur, GA 30033

Downtown Atlanta Senior Services
607 Peachtree St.
Atlanta, GA 30365

Northside Shepherd's Center
425 10th Street NW
Atlanta, GA 30318

North Atlanta Senior Services
3003 Howell Mill Rd. NW
Atlanta, GA 30027

Hawaii

Shepherd's Center
1020 S. Beretania St.
Honolulu, HI 96814

Illinois

Aging Cooperative
700 N. Main
Eureka, IL 61530

NE Rockford Shepherd's Center
Protestant Community Services
227 N. Church St.
Rockford, IL 61101

Indiana

High Street Older Adult Program
219 S. High St.
Muncie, IN 47305

Shepherd's Center
Saint Paul's Church
10 W. 61st St.
Indianapolis, IN 46208

Shepherd's Center at North Church
3803 N. Meridian
Indianapolis, IN 46205

Shepherd's Center
1525 Whitestown Rd.
Zionsville, IN 46077

Iowa

Shepherd's Center
921 Pleasant St.
Des Moines, IA 50309

Kansas

Shepherd's Center
First Presbyterian Church
302 N. 5th St.
Atchison, KS 66002

Kentucky

United Crescent Hill Ministries
1860 Frankfort Ave.
Louisville, KY 40206

Louisiana

Lakeview Area Senior Center
420 Robert E. Lee Blvd.
New Orleans, LA 70124

Uptown Shepherd's Center
6200 St. Charles Ave.
New Orleans, LA 70118

Woodlawn Shepherd's Center
5824 Berkley Dr.
New Orleans, LA 70114

Shepherd's Center
1520 Chickasaw St.
Metairie, LA 70005

Missouri

The Shepherd's Center
5200 Oak St.
Kansas City, MO 64112

Shepherd's Center, S. Kansas City
11800 Holmes
Kansas City, MO 64131

Northtown Shepherd's Center
2018 Gentry St.
Kansas City, MO 64116

Center for New Horizons
1509 W. Truman Rd.
Independence, MO 64050

Shepherd's Center
906 Main
Grandview, MO 64030

Lifelong Learning Center
2739 Mitchell
St. Joseph, MO 64507

Shepherd's Center
P.O. Box 3686 Glenstone Station
Springfield, MO 65804

Downtown Shepherd's Center
1210 Locust St.
St. Louis, MO 63103

Life Enrichment Program
2149 S. Grand
St. Louis, MO 63104

Carondelet Community Betterment Federation
6339 Michigan Ave.
St. Louis, MO 63111

G.W. Trimble House
200 S. Main
Louisiana, MO 63353

New Mexico

Amigos del Valle
Box 4057, Fairview Station
Espanola, NM 87533

New York

Shepherd's Center
250 South St.
Peekskill, NY 10566

Westside Ecumenical Center
165 W. 86th St.
New York, NY 10023

North Carolina

Shepherd's Center
1931 Selwyn Ave.
Charlotte, NC 28207

Hinton Rural Life Center
P.O. Box 27
Hayesville, NC 28904

Downtown Church Center
502 N. Broad
Winston-Salem, NC 27101

Caswell Parish
P.O. Box 639
Yanceyville, NC 27379

Ohio

Shepherd's Center
Wesley United Methodist Church
900 Van Buren
Fostoria, OH 44830

Oklahoma

Shepherd's Center
308 Church St.
Wagoner, OK 74467

Pennsylvania

Comprehensive Care for Senior Adults
Calvary United Methodist Church
48th St. and Baltimore Ave.
Philadelphia, PA 19143

Home Wrap-Around Services
Second Baptist Church
Germantown & Upsala St.
Philadelphia, PA 19119

Vintage, Inc.
401 N. Highland Ave.
Pittsburgh, PA 15206

South Carolina

Shepherd's Center
393 E. Main St.
Spartanburg, SC 29302

Shepherd's Center
226 W. Liberty St.
Sumter, SC 29150

Tennessee

Shepherd's Center
Saint Matthews United Methodist Church
1362 Prescott
Memphis, TN 38111

Texas

Chandler Center
137 W. French Place
San Antonio, TX 78212

Virginia

Shepherd's Center
1205 W. Franklin
Richmond, VA 23220

West Virginia

Shepherd's Center
203 S. Kanawha St.
Beckley, WV 25801

Canada

Shepherd's Center
82 Emma St.
Brockville, Ontario K6V 48R

Interfaith Caregivers Programs
(Robert Wood Johnson Foundation Grants)

Alabama

Area Interfaith Disaster Services
571 Dauphin St.
Mobile, AL 36602

California

Interfaith Service Bureau
3720 Folsom Blvd.
Sacramento, CA 95816

Buenaventura Interfaith Coalition
261 N. Catalina
Ventura, CA 93001

Connecticut

Interfaith Volunteer Caregivers Project
Center Church Parish House
311 Temple St.
New Haven, CT 06511

District of Columbia

Interfaith Conference of Metropolitan Washington
1419 V St., NW
Washington, DC 20009

Guam

Interfaith Volunteer Caregivers Program
P.O. Box 21899 MPO
Guam, GU 96921

Hawaii

Project RESPECT
235 Queen Emma Square
Honolulu, HI 96813

Idaho

Project Interlink
Weisgerber Bldg., Suite 415
5th and Main
Lewiston, ID 83501

Massachusetts

Match-Up
Boston Aging Concerns Committee
67 Newbury St.
Boston, MA 02116

Michigan

> Pontiac Area Lighthouse
> P.O. Box 425
> Pontiac, MI 48056

New Hampshire

> Greater Manchester Coalition
> c/o NH Catholic Charities
> 215 Myrtle St.
> Manchester, NH 03105

New York

> Interfaith Coalition of Northern Manhattan
> c/o NYC Dept. of Health
> 11 Old Broadway
> New York, NY 10027

> Interfaith Volunteer Caregivers Program
> c/o Dept. of Aging
> 255 N. Union St.
> Olean, NY 14760

Ohio

> Interfaith Volunteer Caregivers Project
> 750 Work Dr.
> Akron, OH 44320

> Volunteer Service to Seniors
> 631 Wick Ave.
> Youngstown, OH 44502

Oregon

> Interfaith Volunteer Caregivers Project
> Saint Mary's Church
> 822 Ellsworth SW
> Albany, OR 97321

> Eastern Oregon Community Development Council
> 104 Elm St.
> La Grande, OR 97850

Tennessee

Caregiver's Coalition
1166 A Poplar
Memphis, TN 38173-0130

Texas

Jefferson Area Community Outreach for Older People (CO-OP)
950 Donaldson Ave.
San Antonio, TX 78228

Virginia

Norfolk Interfaith Coalition for the Elderly
820 Colonial Ave.
Norfolk, VA 23507

Washington

Volunteer Chore Ministry
1715 E. Cherry
Seattle, WA 98122

Project S.E.R.V.E.
916 Larson Bldg.
Yakima, WA 98901

Wisconsin

Triniteam, Inc.
First Presbyterian Church
2112 Rudolph Rd
Eau Claire, WI 54701

Interfaith Program for the Elderly
1442 N. Farwell Ave., No. 104
Milwaukee, WI 53202